Kate

For Gary

Thom Smith

Thom Smith

KATE

Published in the United States of America by Leo and Me Publications

Contact the author at: Thom1515@aol.com

Library of Congress Control Number LCCN: 2020907113

ISBN: 978-1-7349197-0-7

eBook ISBN: 978-1-7349197-1-4

BISG-Codes:BIO026000,FIC041000, HIS054000

Printed in the United States of America

*Dedicated to the children of
Kate & Sam Carey*

Preface

The motivation for this book stems from a newspaper article my mother discovered relating to her great-grandmother's death in Rochester, New York, about one hundred years earlier. She shared both the article and her love of genealogy with me, and over the years, I became somewhat obsessed with the story of Kate Carey. Consequently, I felt compelled to document her story for prosperity.

No one else in the family was aware of the circumstances surrounding her death, nor even where she was buried. She left no personal effects behind, not even a photograph, just a mysterious life led and a death that was never discussed.

I began writing this book sometime around 2012 after I'd retired and found myself with (just a little bit) more time on my hands. Initially, I'd devote a few hours a month to the endeavor, mostly during the winter. As time passed, I realized that if I ever wanted to complete this project, and perhaps have it published, I'd need to devote much more time. So, those few hours a month became a few hours per week, but still only in the winter months.

More years passed, as did more relatives.

Finally, in 2019, I gave myself one more year to complete the project and publish it. I've learned so much along the way—about the town I grew up in, the Irish I'm related to, and the respect that these ancestors rightfully deserve.

This historical biography is mostly factual and partially speculation. It falls under the category of creative nonfiction. Every name constitutes a real person, and every date constitutes an actual event that occurred at the time and place indicated. It was written using local newspaper articles, census records, and online searches, all of which are cited in the bibliography.

Prologue

They called me Maggie.

I was born Margaret Elizabeth Leonard, but Maggie seemed like a better fit for most people right from the start. Maybe it was my auburn hair and green eyes that evoked such a lilting Irish nickname. Nevertheless, I went through much of my youth responding to the name Maggie. Or Margaret Elizabeth if either of my parents were upset with me. It was only in my adult life, after my marriage, that I became known as Kate. Kate Carey, to be more specific, which also had a nice Gaelic ring to it. Although, by that time, I was also being called a number of other, less flattering things.

The sad downward spiral of my life began shortly after my marriage to a handsome young Irishman named Samuel Carey. That's when Maggie became Kate. My life deteriorated after our fourth child was born and I realized I had married an abusive alcoholic, or in the language of the day, a man of intemperate habits.

This is the story of where I came from, the thirty-two years I spent on this earth, and the lingering afterlife that was Kate Carey. But it's also a story about water. Yes, water. The lakes, the oceans, and the rivers.

Especially the rivers.

Rivers are the most fluid and dynamic of water bodies. Oceans have currents, but the water in a river is in constant motion and resides in any one location for only a brief moment.

Occasionally, where the topography dictates, rivers manifest themselves into spectacular waterfalls. Very few things in nature can compare to the power of a waterfall, where a river's energy is on continuous display. Only in the relatively short past has man been able to divert and harness some of this power for his own benefit.

Very seldom do rivers die; they seem to be eternal. They bear witness to thousands of years of life around them and the events affected by them. You could say that rivers are the arteries and veins of the earth.

They can sustain life, but they can also take it away.

CHAPTER 1

Geneseo

I was born in the quiet little village of Geneseo in 1852, a town nestled in the fertile Genesee River Valley in the western part of New York State. The town's name evolved from the name of the valley and the river that ran through it. Initially, the first settlement was called Big Tree, after the immense oak tree that stood on the banks of the river nearby. The town was subsequently renamed out of respect for the river, the valley, and its Seneca Indian heritage.

The village, as I knew it, had been in existence since 1790. The Genesee River, on the other hand, was more than twelve thousand years old and originated in a meadow in Potter County, Pennsylvania. At that point, its place of birth, it was just a small meandering brook that you could easily step across. It headed northward, downhill, to eventually empty into the Great Lake known as Ontario, 160 miles away. As it flowed north through New York, it became wider and deeper. It also tumbled over several falls until it passed Rochester and was finally calmed and diluted by the easternmost of the Great Lakes.

But where the river passed Geneseo, there was barely enough incline to keep the stream moving north, giving rise to the local term for that area as "the flats." This characteristic provided the smooth, fertile land so ideal for farming, but it afforded no protection from flooding when the river would swell with heavy rain or melting snow.

As early as I could remember, I'd been fascinated with history. I never got tired of hearing adults tell stories relating to life in the past. I found it fascinating to think about how people lived and what they did before my time. My hunger for learning was seldom satisfied, and I'd ask so many questions that I must have been an annoying little girl to all but the most tolerant adults.

In school, I was taught our town's name was an English version of Jo-nis-hi-yuh, the Seneca term for "beautiful valley." Yet, I couldn't help but notice the similarity of our "white-man's village" called Geneseo with the large Seneca village called *Chenussio*, which had previously existed in the vicinity a century before. My teacher never did give me a satisfactory explanation for that coincidence.

There weren't any Indians living in the town when I grew up there, only stories. Some of those stories were not so pleasant.

The Seneca had sided with the British and the Tories during the American Revolution. After the conflict was over, nearly all of them escaped westward, in fear of reprisals.

About midway through the war, General George Washington sent 3,500 troops into western New York to destroy the Seneca villages and food supplies. General John Sullivan's troops were camped at the southern end of Conesus Lake. They knew they were within a few miles of the largest Seneca village in the area. On the night of September 12, 1779, Sullivan ordered Lieutenant Thomas Boyd to organize a scouting party consisting of twenty-three men, including Sergeant Michael Parker, to discover the village's exact location. The following day, the scouting party was ambushed by a much larger Seneca force, and seventeen men were killed. Several escaped, but Boyd and Parker were captured and taken to Little Beard's Town, the Seneca village they were searching for. The two captives met with a slow, agonizing death at the hands of Chief Little Beard and his warriors.

The scene of their death was just outside the Seneca village on Little Beard's Creek, a small tributary of the Genesee River, just south of Geneseo.

Two days later, Sullivan's army discovered the ambush site, and subsequently, the gruesome remains of Boyd and Parker in the now-empty Seneca village. The village was burned to the ground, and acres of crops were destroyed.

As I say, some of the stories were not pleasant.

That was just one of the many stories I heard from my neighbor, Mr. Silas Whitney. I would spend hours sitting on his front porch, listening to him explain who had lived in this area before we did and how the first pioneers settled the town. Sometimes he'd have a small group of us, including my friends Catherine Houston and Miranda Davis, and his son James, listening intently to his colorful history lessons. But most often, it was just James and me who sat as his captive audience. I think he enjoyed telling these tales as much as we enjoyed listening and imagining what it must have been like.

James Whitney was a year older than me and lived at 71 North Street with his parents and older brother, Charles. His father had purchased the vacant land in 1845 for just over $100 and constructed his house shortly thereafter. Mr. Silas Whitney was somewhat of an inventor and made pumps, right there in a shop behind his house. Occasionally, we'd sit on stools in his shop and listen to him as he worked, but when he was relaxed, sitting on the porch on a summer afternoon, he'd go into great detail on the history of the area.

One particular lazy summer afternoon, he must have been in the mood for a great long story of how our little village came into existence. "In 1852," he began, "the population of Geneseo was just under three thousand, which included newborn Maggie Leonard." He always tried to make the stories personal, so they had more meaning to us. "But," as Mr. Whitney went on to say, "the population, just sixty years earlier, was less than ten."

He said that it all began with the arrival of two brothers from Durham, Connecticut, James and William Wadsworth. "These gentlemen," he went on to say, "were indirectly responsible for my being born here as well." Their father's cousin, Colonel Jeremiah Wadsworth, was one of the wealthiest men in Connecticut after the American Revolution. The colonel had invested with a pair of land speculators named Oliver Phelps and Nathaniel Gorham, who, in 1788, purchased more than two million acres of land in western New York from the Iroquois Confederacy. This vast tract of land was known as the Phelps and Gorham Purchase.

Now they needed land agents, Mr. Whitney explained, to personally move here, survey and improve the land, sell parcels, and promote settlement. Colonel Wadsworth himself purchased two hundred thousand acres in the new territory as an investment. To entice James and William to assist with the endeavor, he offered each of them two thousand acres of prime land at his original cost of eight cents per acre.

They would be allowed to purchase additional land at a reduced rate and would receive a substantial commission for the sale of any of Jeremiah's property. They accepted his proposal and headed west.

The two Wadsworth brothers had distinctly different personalities, functions, and responsibilities. James Wadsworth was a Yale graduate, studious, and served as the planning partner in the relationship. He had a shrewd mind for business deals and was a talented negotiator.

William Wadsworth was more down-to-earth, a working farmer, and considered himself a man with the common touch. He was a rugged, hands-on type and handled the farming aspects of the business. Together they were a highly successful team, and, as the settlement grew, they also served the community in elected supervisory positions.

During the last decade of the eighteenth century, James traveled to New York City, Philadelphia, and Boston to advertise the sale and encourage the settlement of Genesee Valley land. He even sailed to England and the Netherlands to further promote their endeavor.

Back in Geneseo, on August 28, 1797, James and William Wadsworth served as hosts for the Treaty of Big Tree. This treaty effectively extinguished all Indian claims to the land west of the Genesee River and established reservations for the Seneca in New York State.

As the area developed and more settlers arrived, the Wadsworth brothers devoted their time to farming. By 1800, they had acquired over thirty-two thousand acres of the best land. It was once said that a Wadsworth could ride his horse from Geneseo to Rochester and never leave his own land. Subsequently, most of this property was leased to tenant farmers with the option to buy.

The Wadsworths had a great admiration for the stunning oak trees scattered throughout the valley. As they cleared the wilderness, they spared as many as they could. Even when leasing land, they required the tenants to preserve these magnificent trees.

It was during this time that western New York State became sectioned off into counties. The area encompassing Geneseo became Livingston County. With Geneseo being the largest town, and almost geographically centered within the county, it became the county seat. As such, a county courthouse and adjacent jail were built at the north end of town. Gradually the town evolved with all the necessary professions to sustain a growing community: a blacksmith, carriage maker, an innkeeper, and various merchants, along with a gristmill and a machine shop.

By 1832, the village contained two schools, five churches, two banks, a library, and about two thousand inhabitants.

Not only did the Wadsworths help build the population of Geneseo, but they did much to promote the development, enlightenment, and overall betterment of the growing community. James Wadsworth was heavily involved in establishing the first school in Geneseo. The Geneseo Academy, located on Temple Hill on the east side of the village, was erected in 1826. He personally selected a young man to serve as the schoolmaster and paid his wages himself.

Throughout my lifetime, the Wadsworth name remained synonymous with the Genesee Valley, and that legacy would continue far into the future.

The street map of the village, as I knew it, couldn't have been simpler. It was nearly a perfect square, about a mile on each side. North Street and South Street served as their respective sides. Main Street formed the western boundary, and Temple Hill Street formed the parallel eastern side. Center Street ran east and west, bisecting the town in .... the center. Second Street ran north and south, one block east of Main. Third Street, which later became Elm Street, was opened right around the time I was born. It also ran north and south, one block east of Second Street. It wasn't very imaginative but it was simple and easy to understand.

This whole block of a village was set on the side of a gently sloping hill about three hundred feet above the valley floor.

Court Street extended in a westerly direction, from North Street, past the courthouse and down the hill to the river. Before you get to the flats and the river, down at the bottom of Court Street was the train station. The railroad line ran north and south at this point, and the depot and tracks were far enough uphill that they weren't in jeopardy of getting washed away by the spring floods.

Main Street was an actual "street" only between North Street and South Street. Beyond those intersections, it was just a country road. The road headed north to the village of Avon, and south to the towns of Groveland and Mount Morris. Similarly, North, Center, and South Streets continued past the village boundary, but they also quickly turned into country roads with little to see but a few farms. One notable exception was the large, foreboding, three-story brick building about three-quarters of a mile out Center Street, just beyond Hills' Tavern. It was the Livingston County Alms House.

Mr. Whitney told me the complex, as it stood in 1852, was a new and larger version of a structure that, over the years, had proved inadequate for providing protection, shelter, sustenance, and limited care for the insane, the elderly, and the paupers of the surrounding area. This "improved" structure, which stood on 118 acres of land, had just been completed in December of 1850. The surrounding land was used as a farm, which enabled the facility to be as self-sufficient as possible. Consequently, the male inmates carried out as many physical chores as possible, and the female inmates took care of the domestic responsibilities, whenever possible. This degree of self-reliance lessened the financial burden on the county coffers.

When I first laid eyes on this ominous structure, little did I realize the impact it would have on my life and the lives of my future children.

Like most towns, our Main Street had always been the heart of Geneseo. There was a village green at the southern end, and the courthouse held a prominent position at the northern end. It was visible from just about anywhere along the street. Like bookends, the two Wadsworth estates were built at either end of Main Street, with the business district as the centerpiece.

William Wadsworth settled in the south, and his estate became known as "The Homestead." The houses were grander and more elaborate in this part of town. The farther you got from the southwest corner, the smaller and poorer-looking the houses became. Unfortunately, we lived at the complete opposite edge of town, about as far away from the luxury and wealth as we could be. But we were a happy and hardworking family and grateful to live in the land of opportunity.

The James Wadsworth family established their estate, known as Hartford House, at the north end of Main Street. But it was much further outside the village, almost as if they needed more room between them and the families on the north side of town. We lived at the upper end of North Street, near the corner of North and Temple Hill Street. Mr. Whitney told us that North Street was originally called Mulberry Street because of the large number of mulberry bushes that grew there. Only a few mulberry trees were left now, but my girlfriends and I would spend many a summer afternoon gathering the dark purple berries to bring home to our mothers. Sometimes we ate as many as would survive the trip home, but I always made sure Mother would have enough to make a pie.

When the village was still young, North Street was mostly pasture and orchards. There were only a few small tenant houses and a distillery. More houses were built as the village grew. Smaller houses from the southern portion of the village were moved there, replaced by larger homes and wealthy owners. But an abundance of fruit trees remained behind almost every house on the street, providing a generous supply of free food for the poorer families on the north side of town.

At the south end of Main Street, the village green, or town square, was set aside by the Wadsworths for use by the town. It was a large open area of about fifteen acres. Over the years, it had been the home of a wide variety of activities, from circuses to sporting competitions. Unfortunately, it would also be used for less joyful events such as military drills. Mr. Whitney had, one day, given me the history of this now-familiar park.

Several years before I was born, Miss Elizabeth Wadsworth, the youngest of the five children born to James and Naomi Wadsworth, took it upon herself to beautify the town square. She planted rare and beautiful trees, put in flower beds and gravel footpaths, and enclosed it all with a lovely fence. She granted it to the village for use in perpetuity as a park. Unfortunately, after her death, the year before I was born, it fell into disrepair and quickly became overgrown with weeds. I can recall seeing cattle, sheep, and swine grazing there as a young child. Ultimately, embarrassment and moral conscience took hold, and the village passed an ordinance banning livestock from the park, and it was once again brought back to its original beauty. But that didn't happen until I had become a married woman.

Many beautiful buildings lined Main Street. A glorious concert hall at the south end, several hotels and boarding houses, a bank, a church, the Big Tree Lodge, many businesses, and several magnificent homes. These gems were capped with the stately courthouse at the north end.

To me, it was the grandest village a person would ever want to grow up in. I was grateful that my parents had settled here. I was also thankful for such a valuable resource as Mr. Whitney, so close at hand, to provide its history and answer my questions.

CHAPTER 2

Genesee River and Transportation

One chilly autumn day, sitting by the stove in Mr. Whitney's workshop, we talked about the river that flowed past our town. I had never thought of it as more than a short section of water that formed convoluted loops across the flats. But I learned that afternoon that it was much more than I had ever envisioned.

The Genesee River flowed northward, through the valley, to the city of Rochester, where it emptied into Lake Ontario. Rochester was about thirty miles from Geneseo as the crow flies, but if one followed the river, the distance traveled would be closer to ninety miles. That provides an indication as to how many twists and turns the river took. In fact, there are several stretches where it takes big turns and actually flows south before rounding another big bend and returning to a northerly flow.

It was far from a straightforward path. Much like my life would end up being.

It was a good thing the village was established up the hill from the river because occasionally there would be some terrible flooding, especially in the springtime, down in the valley. There were times when the flats themselves looked like a "great lake." The river provided both fertility to the valley and a means of transportation to the city of Rochester. But it also provided death and destruction on a routine basis. Sadly, it was due to the riverbank's constant erosion that we would ultimately lose our landmark "Big Tree."

Trade and transportation between the towns in the Genesee Valley and Rochester's port depended on the height and flow of the river. Early on, traveling north from Geneseo to Rochester would generally take about two days. However, the return trip, going upstream, might require four or five days. With the introduction of steam-powered vessels, the trip was shortened to less than a day in either direction. A rear-wheeled steamboat called the *Genesee* would leave Geneseo at five in the morning and be in Rochester before noon. The return trip would leave Rochester at 4 p.m. and reach Geneseo before midnight. Unfortunately, it only lasted a few seasons and was soon replaced by the railroad.

Transportation between Rochester and towns to the south became considerably easier and more efficient when rail lines were built in the valley. That happened soon after I was born. Travel by team and wagon, in particular stagecoaches, gradually became less attractive but never completely disappeared like the steamboat did.

Although the railroad was a blessing to travelers, it meant the demise of at least one local business.

On upper Center Street, Hills' Tavern was ideally situated on the main stage route that ran from Canandaigua in the east, to Buffalo in the west. Erastus Hills, the tavern's owner, had died in 1844, before the coming of the rail line, but his widow, Rosina, and their seven children carried on the business. However, with fewer customers because of the decrease in stage travel, the family needed to close the tavern in 1861. The widow Hills died a few years later, and none of the children had the desire to re-establish what they considered an obsolete endeavor. One of the youngest daughters, Mary Hills, had become the most resentful member of the family at the loss of her family's business. She felt bitter about progress if it meant the demise of a family's livelihood, and focused her anger on the town's leaders. She became so rancorous that she lived the rest of her life without leaving the property. At her request, her remains were buried at Temple Hill, just a few hundred yards from the tavern, so that even her corpse wouldn't travel into the village.

In addition to river and rail, roads between Geneseo and Rochester were generally decent. A stagecoach made the trip on a daily basis at a lower cost but traveled at a considerably slower pace than the railroad. Anyone with a horse and carriage could make their way to the city, over easy terrain, in a day's time.

The proximity and ease of travel between Geneseo and Rochester would ultimately have an impact on my life and death.

CHAPTER 3

Ireland

I was the fourth child born to John and Catherine Leonard. They grew up and were married in Galway County, Ireland. That's also where my oldest brother and sister, Michael and Mary, were born. My sister Catherine was born in England in 1851 on the family's journey to America, fleeing the devastation of the Great Famine.

It was ironic that what brought my parents to such a fertile land was a potato disease that completely destroyed the primary food crop they had grown up with.

My parents never spoke to me about what it was like growing up in Ireland. It must have been a tough existence, and they may have wanted to forget that part of their life. It was only through gathering snippets of conversation between them, and generalizations in response to my questions, that I tried to fit together the pieces of their childhoods. I'd hear them talk about their time in Galway, but I also heard them reflect on their friends and family in Tipperary. Since those two counties were adjacent to one another, I suppose they could have lived near the border. I'm not sure exactly where they were born in Ireland, and I regret that I never asked, but Mother would tell me stories about the country they came from and the perilous journey to America. I never tired of these stories and learning about their homeland.

County Galway was a rather mountainous region of Ireland, certainly more rugged than the gently rolling hills of western New York. But there was a similarity with the presence of a large number of lakes in both regions. County Galway was home to several of the largest lakes in Ireland. Similarly, east of the Genesee Valley was a series of long, narrow lakes running north and south, known as the Finger Lakes. These were formed by retreating glaciers that left deep gouges in the land, which subsequently filled with water.

County Tipperary was located in the central plain of Ireland, but it also contained several mountain ranges. The River Suir flowed through the southern portion of the county, and tributaries of the River Shannon drained the northern section. The county's center was known as the "Golden Vale," a fertile area of land in the Suir basin, not unlike the Genesee Valley. Perhaps the similarity in climate and geography eased my parents' and older siblings' transition when they settled here.

One thing was for sure, my parents were both devoted Roman Catholics, and they were grateful to have survived not only the Great Famine in their homeland but also the voyage to America.

The Great Famine, or the Great Hunger as it was sometimes called back in Ireland, began around 1845. Mother would go into abundant detail when she'd relate stories about it. It lasted almost seven years, and during that time, over a million died from starvation or disease, and a million more fled the country. One-quarter of the population left the Emerald Isle for even greener pastures.

It wasn't until I attended school that I learned why the loss of a single vegetable had such an impact on an entire country. This famine was so devastating because almost half the population was reliant solely on the potato as a primary food source, especially during the winter. In 1845, two-thirds of all the Irish tenant farms were so small that no crop other than potatoes would yield enough to feed a family. Tenant farmers worked for their landlords in return for a small patch of land where they could grow enough food for their own family. With such dim prospects and dependence upon a single crop's survival, the lure of huge parcels of rich, fertile land in America was extremely enticing–even if it meant continuing to work as a tenant farmer for someone else. Although the sea voyage to America was rumored to be long and difficult, the potential rewards seemed to far outweigh the risk.

The year my parents decided to leave their homeland for America, they joined 250,000 fellow countrymen and relatives.

Early in 1850, my parents, in their early twenties, with a two-year-old son and a newborn baby girl, headed for England hoping to gain passage on a less expensive, less crowded--and thereby safer ship. Horror stories had filtered back to potential emigrants about the "coffin ships" that were transporting hordes of refugees to North America from the harbors of western Ireland. Of the estimated one hundred thousand Irish that sailed to Canada in 1847, about 20 percent died from disease and malnutrition during the voyage or shortly thereafter. The ships that left the unregulated ports of western Ireland were overcrowded, poorly maintained, and badly provisioned. The grim choice for many was whether to die of starvation at home or at sea.

The American author Ralph Waldo Emerson, whose life span was approximately the same duration and timeframe as my father's, said, "The road from Liverpool to New York, as they who have traveled it well know, is very long, crooked, rough, and eminently disagreeable." It's highly unlikely that Mr. Emerson made the voyage packed in the hold of a cargo ship like thousands of Irish immigrants did, so his quote is something of an understatement.

Most of the ships were bound for the port cities of Boston, New York, Philadelphia, and Baltimore. The vast majority of those immigrants making the voyage elected to stay in these cities because they had either run out of money, were too tired or ill to continue on, or simply lacked the initiative after such a grueling journey. But those who were determined to return to a more pastoral life headed for the rural interiors of the northeastern states. This additional transportation required more money or indenture to some wealthy landowner.

The cost of a transatlantic voyage varied significantly and depended on the ship, time of year, additional cargo, and the number of passengers. Father found the cheapest passage available, with the best chance of survival, to be about 70 shillings per person or about 14 pounds for the whole family.[1]

My father sold all the family furniture and what possessions they could part with to raise money for the voyage. He found it was just enough to purchase a reasonable passage for his family with very little leftover to start a new life in America. They made their way to the Port of Galway and boarded a ship headed for Liverpool, England.

---

[1] That would be equivalent to approximately $17 per person in today's U.S. dollars. About $70 for a family of four.

Shortly after arriving in England, my mother discovered she was pregnant again. Although there were many transportation options to America, my parents couldn't afford the newer steamships that made the transatlantic voyage in about two weeks. Even if they could obtain tickets for third class, more commonly known as steerage, it would have meant being forced into the belly of the ship along with hundreds of others for the fourteen-day duration. And that number didn't even include the rats, mice, and other vermin that made the voyage with the human cargo.

The alternative mode of transportation was the clipper ship and was significantly more affordable. Although the journey could take as long as six weeks, three times longer than by steamship, Father felt that the conditions would be more bearable for his young family. However, not wanting to risk having his third child born at sea, he decided it would be wise to wait in England until the baby was born. So it was that their third child, a baby girl, was born in England at the beginning of 1851. They named her Catherine after my mother. She joined her older brother, Michael, who was now three years old, and their sister, Mary, still an infant herself.

During this time in England, my father heard about the opportunities being offered by agents of the Wadsworth family. The generosity of the Wadsworth family reached far and wide. In a humanitarian effort, arrangements could be made to help defray the cost of the transatlantic voyage, for those affected by the Great Famine in Ireland, in return for their labor on the Genesee Valley farms.

As the head of a family of five who was not opposed to working the soil, my father jumped at the opportunity offered by the Wadsworths. In the spring of 1851, the family departed Liverpool on their way to Boston, Massachusetts.

Mr. Wadsworth's agents also arranged for overland transportation from Boston to the fertile valley of the Genesee. So, the family set sail for Boston Harbor, arriving there in July, after a short layover in Halifax, Nova Scotia.

Once again, my mother discovered she was pregnant. However, this time, my father decided they would make the trip to western New York since it would be less perilous for all concerned.

So it was that my first breaths were not of the cool mist of the Irish countryside, nor salty sea air, nor even the dense, fish-laden atmosphere of Boston Harbor, but of the sweet, fragrant air of the Seneca Indian's beautiful valley.

CHAPTER 4

First Years in Geneseo

Catholics were as scarce as Indians in my family's new hometown. What few Catholics there were, prior to our arrival, would gather for mass and religious services at either the concert hall, the courthouse, or a similar facility. As the town grew, so did the resentment toward permitting the use of public buildings for Catholic services. Ultimately a ban was imposed that forced worshipers to hold services at the homes of congregation members. It wasn't unusual to see parishioners kneeling in the front yard or on the sidewalk of a private home on Sunday mornings. But thanks, once again, to the generosity of James Wadsworth, we were able to establish our own church. He donated a plot of land at the foot of North

Street and loaned $500 to construct the building. Under Reverend Father Maguire, a modest church was erected, and, in 1854, Saint Mary's parish was established.

Father worked long days on Mr. Wadsworth's farm. He'd get picked up before dawn by a wagon full of men and delivered home just in time for supper. During his first season, the fields were just getting back to yielding decent harvests. The previous year, the wheat crop had been almost entirely destroyed by a weevil. I'm sure it crossed my father's mind that perhaps he was about to witness another agricultural apocalypse.

Around this time, our valley lost the massive oak tree for which the town was originally named. The "Big Tree," former site of a Seneca village and title of the treaty that relinquished those Indian lands, was taken by the river.

Torrents of rain on Saturday, November 7, 1857, resulted in the worst flooding the valley had seen in twenty years. The next day, no longer able to withstand the rushing floodwaters that ate away at its base, the Big Tree became another victim of the river. Fortunately, a large section of the lower trunk was salvaged and kept for prosperity and future generations to marvel at its size and significance. At the time, the tree was believed to be more than three hundred years old. I was only five when this happened and don't remember it, but Mr. Whitney told me the story several years later. What a landmark to have lost, and by something as seemingly harmless as water.

As our church was being built at the bottom of North Street, our family was living in a modest house at the top of the street. Although I don't remember it feeling so at the time, it must have been crowded for a family of six. And it was shortly thereafter that the family grew to seven, and before long, ten.

I was a one-year-old baby when my sister Elizabeth was born. Not until I was six years old did I have my first distinct memory of growing up in that house. That year, 1858, Mama gave birth to twin girls. I remember the chaos in our tiny dwelling the morning she went into labor. The fear, the moans of pain, and the relief of hearing new babies cry left a lasting impression on my young mind.

My new baby sisters were Anna and Ellen, and I felt a sense of importance that I could help Mama by taking care of things in the house while she rested. Of course, my older sisters were also there to help, and I'm sure they did much more than I did. I helped wash clothes but was not allowed to do any ironing or cooking. By the time I was seven years old, my baby brother, John, had joined the family, which meant even more laundry to do on wash day. But it was a chore I was happy to help with. One concept my parents impressed upon us was that we may be poor by some standards, but there was no excuse for not being clean. Soap and water were cheap. We never wore tattered or dirty clothing and maintained a sense of pride in that.

One sunny morning in June of 1860, a man stopped at our house to gather information for the federal census. Father was at work, and Michael was helping the neighbors, so it was just Mama, baby John, and us six girls at home. He introduced himself as Mr. Lauderdale, and seeing that my mother had her hands full, assured her that his interview would be as brief as possible. Mama was able to answer all of his questions while I sat and listened attentively. I wanted to learn all I could about this thing called a census. Mr. Lauderdale must have thought it was cute, or possibly annoying, that I started asking him my own questions. Still curious, I followed him down the street as he gathered information at each house. I'd wait in the front yard as he entered the homes and asked his questions. When he finished with one house, we'd move on to the next one. I felt useful, introducing him to each of my neighbors, although I'm sure he was just being polite when he told me how much he appreciated my help.

Miss Lucinda Thompson and her son, Joseph, lived two houses away. They were Negroes, and Miss Thompson did housework for other people. Joe Thompson was a quiet boy, about six years older than me, and would sometimes walk with us to school. Father didn't like that, and I heard him telling Mama that it would lead to trouble. But Joe Thompson didn't seem to go to school that often, so there was never a problem. I'm not sure what he did all day, but he wasn't in school.

My best friend, Catherine Houston, lived next door to the Thompsons. She was my age and we looked a lot alike. Some people thought we were sisters. Her father was a gardener and had come from Ireland as well, and her mom's name was Margaret. We had a lot in common; maybe that's why

I liked her so much. She had a couple of younger brothers too, but nobody's family on the street was as large as ours.

Just past Catherine's house was the home of my other close friend, Miranda Davis. She was a year younger but was smarter than all the kids we played with. Her father owned a store on Main Street, and they had the biggest, most beautiful house on the street.

I decided to stay at Miranda's house and let the census taker continue on without my assistance. Catherine joined us, and we wandered into her backyard where there was a lovely cherry tree loaded with ripe cherries. We climbed into the tree and ate cherries as I watched the census taker until he was out of sight.

He had already been to my other friends' houses on the street: Josephine Hull, Sarah Fowler, and James Whitney. They were all just a little bit older than I was. Sarah Fowler was born in England, and although she was only ten, she worked as a servant for George and Mary Whitney. My friend James Whitney, who was nine, lived next door to them at 71 North Street with his parents and older brother, Charles. His father, Silas, had been an endless source of stories and local history for the past two years. He also had a servant girl living in his house. Her name was Margaret McLeod. She was from Scotland and was sixteen.

Life was pleasant and peaceful that summer for an eight-year-old girl whose main concerns were not falling out of a tree or eating too many sour cherries. But I could sense growing anxieties among some of the adults on our street.

CHAPTER 5

A Year
of Tension

There was a lot of controversy in 1860
about the growing tensions in the southern
states over Negro slaves. We even discussed
it in school. But now that school had ended
for the summer, I thought the topic might
fade away. Quite the contrary, the adults
seemed to become more obsessed with it.

The only Negroes I knew were Joe
and Miss Thompson. They were nice folks
and owned their own home. Miss
Thompson worked hard, and for several
people, but I never thought of her as
anyone's slave. On the other hand, my
friend Sarah Fowler was a white girl who
seemed to be owned by the Whitney family.
She worked for them in return for room and

board, which I suppose was almost like being a slave.

Very confusing concepts for an eight-year-old Irish girl.

I remembered our schoolteacher telling us that as early as 1837, the town of Geneseo had formed an anti-slavery society known as The Friends of Universal Freedom. This group reflected the opinions of the majority of the townspeople, who were very much opposed to the concept of slavery and were staunch abolitionists.

The year 1860 was also a year to elect a new president, and the campaigns of all four parties were in full swing that summer. The Republican Party seemed the strongest with Abraham Lincoln and Hannibal Hamlin leading the ticket. The Democratic Party had put forth Stephen Douglas and Herschel Johnson, and an offshoot of that party, the Seceders, had proposed John Breckinridge and Joseph Lane. A fourth party, the Constitutional Union, was running John Bell and Edward Everett for the top positions.

On one of those lazy summer afternoons, sitting on Mr. Whitney's porch and listening to him explain politics to

James and me, he told us about an
organization in town called the Wide
Awakes, which was affiliated with the
Republican Party. They were part of a
larger, nationwide organization estimated to
include over four hundred thousand
members. He told us that they served as
political police and bodyguards for the
Republican Party. Membership was
restricted to males over the age of eighteen.
Although their intentions may have been
honorable initially, I'm sure they were an
intimidating force to be reckoned with and
possibly swayed more than a few voters.
The group in Geneseo would rally at night
and march through town, wearing long
robes or capes and carrying six-foot torches.
It was quite a sight to behold.

Overall, the summer of 1860 was
exceedingly memorable for me.

On the Fourth of July, the town held
a big celebration with a parade, marching
bands, and firework displays. There was a
large gathering of families for a pic nic[2] at
Long Point Park on Conesus Lake. This lake
was the westernmost of the Finger Lakes

---

[2] The term "picnic" was spelled this way during the mid-
nineteenth century. Later in the century it was combined as
one word.

and the closest one to Geneseo. My brother Michael, my sisters Mary and Catherine, and I rode to the park with James Whitney and his family. Among the festivities, Company A of the Big Tree Artillery, part of the local militia, held a target practice. They fired their cannons at targets floating on small barges on the lake. The demonstration soon turned into a contest of accuracy, with wagers being made by several of the participants. Fortunately for our group, James' Uncle George won the contest, which made the ride back to Geneseo all that more enjoyable.

It was a joyful time to spend with James and his family. None of us could have imagined that his mother would be gone in a matter of months.

Similarly, little did I realize that the frequency of happy years in my own life would become fewer and fewer. My future was destined to become a series of peaks and valleys, not unlike the rolling hills of the surrounding terrain. But in the mind of a young girl, things were just fine in Geneseo that summer, and in my life, and they would be for as long as I could envision.

My father was working hard at Mr. Wadsworth's farm, six days a week. The crops were all doing fine that summer as well. There was no evidence of disease or devastation by the weevils or any other pest. There was an abundant crop of winter barley and Genesee wheat. By the end of July, it had all been cut and harvested. The fruit trees, including those behind our house, were laden with apples, pears, and peaches. The corn crop was running a little late, but it was healthy and robust, and by August should be ready to eat.

School began at the end of August, and to celebrate, there was another gala picnic at Long Point Park. It was a large event with about two thousand children and one thousand adults in attendance, representing thirty-two different schools. It was an exciting occasion, marking the beginning of another school year.

Our schoolhouse was a cobblestone building about halfway up Center Street. It was built in 1838 and served as the primary schoolhouse for Genesee District No. 5 for the next hundred years.

By September of 1860, much of the town had new gas lighting installed in the houses, businesses, and along many of the streets. There were gas lampposts along the entire lengths of Main, South, and Second

Streets. They extended up a portion of Center and North Streets but nowhere near our house. In fact, I could barely see the lampposts lit at the foot of the hill, even on the darkest night. Those were the nights when the stars twinkled brighter, and the excitement of capturing fireflies in a mason jar was far more enlightening than a glaring streetlamp. I enjoyed being out at night during the warmer months. My two older sisters and I would often just wander down North Street, observing the warm glow and silhouettes from the windows of houses beyond our neighborhood.

It was after dark on Election Day that we heard townspeople spreading the news that Abraham Lincoln would be our new president. The following day, the Wide Awakes held a celebratory parade in the afternoon and a torchlight procession through the village that night.

However, most of the joy in our neighborhood was overshadowed by the death of James Whitney's mother only a few days prior. As we mourned their loss, my parents did what they could to help ease the sorrow of her surviving husband and two sons.

This was the first time I had experienced death on a personal level. She was the first person to die that I was friends with and talked with every week. The feeling of sadness and permanent loss would stay with me for years.

CHAPTER 6

A Country Divided

During the winter of 1860, tensions were growing stronger over the views and policies of the southern states and the newly elected officials in the north. President Lincoln was trying to keep the Union together, but five days before Christmas, South Carolina seceded from the Union.

Within two months, six more southern states had joined them, and by February 1861, The Confederate States of America was formed with Jefferson Davis as their president. It seemed inevitable that the growing hostility between these two "countries" would ultimately lead to an actual conflict. This prompted the Big Tree Artillery unit, situated in town, to begin drills and firing practice twice a week in preparation for any potential hostility.

James Samuel Wadsworth, son of the town's founder, was expected to inherit and continue his father's legacy. Although he attended both Harvard and Yale Universities, obtained a law degree, and was admitted to the bar, he had no desire to start a law practice, but instead entered politics.

When it became apparent that an actual war with the Confederate States may be unavoidable, he joined the Union army with a commission as a major general in the New York State Militia. Realizing that the conflict could be a long and costly one, he began recruiting men from Livingston County to form at least one complete regiment. To provide barracks and training grounds for these troops, a camp was established at the top of North Street, only a few hundred yards from our house. The site was called Camp Union, and before long, it was filled with more than seven hundred men.

The regiment was named the Wadsworth Guards, and they trained under the command of Colonel John Rorbach. This unit would ultimately become the 104th New York Volunteers when called into action. That call appeared to be getting closer when Confederate forces began shelling Fort Sumter in Charleston Harbor off the coast of South Carolina, on April 12, 1861.

War had begun.

Within six weeks, four more states seceded from the Union to join the Confederacy.

There was a flurry of activity on North Street that spring. Wagons and troops regularly traversed our street between Camp Union and the train depot at the bottom of Court Street. It was an unsettling sight to watch cannons, caissons, and limbers wheeling their way up our previously tranquil street of small, modest homes and fruit trees. Musket and cannon fire on the practice field, within a half-mile of my house, sounded as if an actual battle had begun in our peaceful valley. The smell of gunpowder smoke slowly drifted over the neighborhood, overwhelming the more familiar aromas of baking bread or spring flowers. I no longer heard birds in the woods behind our home.

On July 21 of 1861, the first major land battle of the growing conflict between the United States and the Confederate States broke out. Citizens in the North wanted our army to march into Richmond, Virginia, the capital of the Confederacy, and put a quick end to this uprising. The Union generals led their troops, which had been stationed around Washington, across a shallow river known as Bull Run, into Virginia. They quickly encountered Confederate troops camped near the town of Manassas Junction, just twenty-five miles southwest of Washington.

Both armies were equally inexperienced. Union troops initiated the attack, but it was poorly organized, and the rebels put up more of a fight than anticipated. Confederate reinforcements quickly turned the battle into a rout, and the Union troops withdrew back to Washington. The retreat was more of a panicked, disorganized run.

Those of us in the North referred to this first major conflict as the Battle of Bull Run, while the South called it the Battle of Manassas. Interesting that they associated it with the town and civilization, while we named it after the natural landmark, a river.

Both armies realized the sobering reality of war and that this conflict wasn't going to end quickly or easily. There was a total of almost 900 men killed and 2,600 wounded during this first confrontation.

Even a nine-year-old girl could see that there was nothing "civil" about this Civil War.

Back home in Geneseo, a proclamation was made that any able-bodied young men should enlist by July 31 or be subject to a fine of three dollars to help offset the cost of building the regiment. An additional fine of seventy-five cents would be levied and would go to the town. By the end of October, there were about four hundred men at the camp, with the formation of seventeen new companies for the Wadsworth Guards. Additional barracks and a guardhouse were constructed before winter arrived.

The government supplied uniforms and outerwear, but a call went out for wool socks and warmer undergarments in anticipation of the war extending into the winter. My mother felt bad about not being able to help with this request, but she barely had enough to clothe and feed our family of ten.

Camp Union was growing and becoming busier than ever. From our porch, I'd watch a seemingly endless parade of troops and wagons generating dust clouds as they traveled up and down North Street. The sound of countless soldiers' boots and horses' hooves reverberated in my chest.

With so many men confined in such a relatively small space, there was concern over the safety and sensitivities of the neighboring townspeople. A decree established that no liquor would be allowed in camp, and anyone caught with spirits of any sort would be fined seventy-five cents. There was even a fine for swearing. Any soldier heard swearing would be fined one dollar per swear. The policy of the camp was that men could not be soldiers unless they were gentlemen. Mother was pleased with these rules, having the camp so close to our house. I'm sure it lessened her anxiety, having her family, including six young girls, in such close proximity to hundreds of men.

Even though I was only nine, I personally knew a few of the men that enlisted with this recent call to arms and were training at the camp.

James Whitney had two eighteen-year-old cousins who both joined the army on October 2, 1861. Isaac and Lorenzo Whitney enlisted as privates in the 104th Infantry Regiment and were assigned to Company C. I had gotten to know Isaac and Lorenzo as they would occasionally join James and me on the front porch, listening to their uncle Silas's stories. Had it not been that James was only thirteen, I feared that he might have enlisted right along with them.

James Luce was also eighteen and enlisted on the same day, in the same regiment. He enlisted along with his father, Warren, who was forty-four, and they became privates in Company D. James Luce was the boyfriend of Margaret McLeod, the seventeen-year-old servant girl for Silas Whitney. I knew Margaret from our days on the porch, and James would occasionally call on her while I was there. She told me in private how much she loved James and wanted to marry him, but they decided to wait until after the war was over.

On the day these men enlisted, it began raining, and it continued to rain for three days straight. This was by far the most amount of steady rain that I had witnessed in my short lifetime. The river quickly overflowed its banks, and the fields along the river were covered with four to ten feet of water. After the rain stopped, many of us from the neighborhood walked down to the depot to observe the spectacle for ourselves. The air was heavy with the smell of mud and moisture, and the sky was still gray.

The valley looked like a giant lake, larger even than Conesus Lake.

It was later reported that some cattle and hundreds of sheep that had been grazing in the valley were lost. There was also considerable damage to most of the bridges in the area. Some, like the one over the river in Mount Morris, were completely washed away.

Once again, the river, so critical to our community's livelihood, reminded us that it could also deal us death and destruction.

Monday, October 21, I awoke to the first frost of the season and the shocking news that my friend James Whitney had died.

He was only thirteen.

He hadn't been feeling well for several days and stayed home from school the previous week. His father told mine that James had an inflammation of his gut, and he thought it might develop into something serious. The doctor examined him on Saturday and gave him some medicine, but told Mr. Whitney that he thought his recovery was doubtful. Early Monday morning, he peacefully slipped away.

I couldn't bring myself to attend school after I heard the news. Mother told me it was alright to stay home until I felt like I could cope with the loss of my dear friend.

Later that week, I read the announcement of his death in the newspaper, and it rekindled those raw emotions I'd felt on Monday. Among the kind words it had about his short life, the notice in the *Livingston Republican* read, "When it became evident that he could not long survive, his father conversed with him about dying. He listened with calmness, twice repeating the Lord's Prayer, and earnestly prayed that he might meet his beloved mother in heaven."

I cried myself to sleep that night.

CHAPTER 7

The War
Hits Home

There had been a lull in the war during the fall of 1861. Nothing much happened for several months, in fact. I had enough emptiness and sorrow in my heart that I didn't need additional news of our soldiers being killed around the country. Especially the local boys I knew and worried about.

The call for recruits continued.

Several new companies began training at Camp Union. Almost five hundred men enlisted with eight new companies, each consisting of fifty to eighty-five men. As an enticement, those enlisting would receive between thirteen and twenty-three dollars per month, plus a one-hundred-dollar bounty at the end of the war.

Apparently, this incentive proved attractive to many local farmers who were beginning to face the winter season with little revenue. Perhaps they optimistically thought the war would be over by spring, and this could supplement their income in the meantime. But a bleak winter season locally paled in comparison to the continued challenges in Ireland.

On December 19, 1861, the *Livingston Republican* reported on the unrelenting famine in Ireland. The article noted that "not more than one-fourth of the potato crop is available for human food...Surely this terrible condition of the Green Isle is worse than even the evils of civil war." Conditions had not improved much since Father decided to bring his family to America. We were all grateful that he took that bold step, even though we were now living in a country at war with itself.

In January of 1862, there was a flurry of activity at Camp Union. The top of North Street was never busier. Ninety more men had enlisted in the Wadsworth Guards, which necessitated the construction of four new barracks and a hospital. Each company of the guard marched six miles a day. There were in-camp drills every morning and a dress parade each evening. We could hear these drills daily, and it was a constant reminder that our country was still at war.

As if the war was not worrisome enough, in early February, we learned that there had been an outbreak of diphtheria in the town of Lima, about ten miles to the northeast of us. It was reported that nearly two hundred cases were identified in that town alone. Most of the deaths had been children under ten. As someone in that age bracket, this threat was suddenly a cause for concern and not taken lightly. I was afraid I would get sick and die. The loss of my friend Jim Whitney was still fresh in my mind.

The day before Valentine's Day, rumors started to circulate that one of the soldiers at Camp Union had died. The initial fear was that diphtheria had finally reached our town. But it was subsequently confirmed that he had died of measles. Any time a soldier dies, it's a sad situation, but Mother and Father breathed a sigh of relief when they heard diphtheria was not the cause.

This was the first person to have died while at the camp, but it was not the last of the death notices that month.

During the last week of February, our newspaper reported the death of President Lincoln's young son. William Wallace Lincoln, known as Willie, died on February 20, at the age of eleven.

He was only a year older than I was.

He died from typhoid fever, which was usually contracted from contaminated food or water. The water supply for the White House was drawn from the Potomac River, upon whose banks thousands of soldiers and horses were camped. It could be argued that the river was responsible for young Willie's death.

On February 26, 1862, the entire regiment that had been training at Camp Union, departed for the war. Approximately seven hundred men left the camp, marched through the streets of the village, and continued down the hill to the railroad depot. They were led in this procession by McArthur's Brass Band. The parade allowed most of the village to observe the regiment in full uniform and bid them farewell. Situated right at the starting point of the procession, my entire family gathered in the yard with front row seats to see them off. Although it was cold, the sun shone brightly off the instruments in the marching band. It even reflected off the shiny brass buttons on the dark blue overcoats of the soldiers.

Once at the train station, the band continued to play as the troops boarded the extended line of wooden cars that would take them to Rochester and eventually on to Washington.

By the end of March, a mere four weeks after the soldiers departed, all of the buildings and furnishings at Camp Union were auctioned off and dismantled for lumber. There was little evidence that an army camp of nearly a thousand men was ever at that spot. It was also a sign of optimism in my young mind that we would no longer need to train troops and send them off to war.

Locally, diphtheria remained our biggest concern. In May, there was an outbreak in Livonia, which resulted in the death of five children in just one week. In June, five more children died from the disease in Avon, and three in Geneseo. Mama was scared and took extra precautions to keep us away from anyone who may have been in contact with a case of it. We prayed each night that we would all remain healthy.

Just before our summer recess from school, I had become friends with a girl named Catherine Bogy. She was a year younger than me, and her brother James was a year older. They also had two older brothers and an older sister who weren't in school. There were lots of similarities between her family and mine. Her father's name was John, her mother was Margaret, like me, and her name was Catherine, like my mother. Her parents and older siblings had been born in Ireland, like mine, and they moved here to escape the famine as my family had. They settled in Geneseo a year before we did.

Catherine was a kind girl, but she seemed rather sad most of the time, and she missed a lot of school. She confided in me that her father would sometimes beat her mother and the children when he got drunk. I had noticed bruises on her arms before but had never asked her about them. I sensed that she was ashamed and embarrassed about how they got there. I felt terrible for her and her family. It must have been a miserable existence to be afraid of your own father.

I wasn't too surprised when I read the news of her mother's death one July morning. There were a lot of rumors and gossip as to the cause of her death, but the only thing known for certain was that her body was found in the river.

I wondered what would become of Catherine, James, and the other children. The eldest brother, William, was twenty and had enlisted in the 33rd Regiment. He was away fighting in the war. The eldest daughter, Bridget, was seventeen, and I assumed she'd take responsibility for bringing up the other children. John was fourteen, James was eleven, and Catherine was nine. The article in the newspaper wasn't pleasant, but I read it several times, each time my eyes brimmed with tears, and I felt a little sick to my stomach as I envisioned what I read.

The July 10, 1862, issue of the *Livingston Republican* reported it this way:

> On Sunday morning last, the body of the wife of John Bogy was found in the river a mile or so above where Big Tree formally stood. She left home on Wednesday of last week, and no trace of her could be

discovered until her body was found as described. The body presented a most sickening sight, it being bloated to more than double its usual size, and as it was removed from the water, the hair and scalp all came off. We understand that a few days before her disappearance, she and her husband had a quarrel in which he gave her a severe beating. He is very intemperate, and will work but very little, and what little he earns is usually spent for whiskey, the family depending on the efforts of the mother for subsistence. On the inquest, which was held by Coroner Ames, of Mount Morris, a daughter testified that her mother drank some, and that of late she had been a good deal excited about a son in Capt. Warford's Company. For the last year, this son has aided his mother considerably. Her death is undoubtedly traceable to whiskey, and the love of money must be strong

with any man who would sell
Bogy whiskey—at best, he is
but a poor miserable creature.

I thought to myself, as well, what a
horrible beast this John Bogy must be. He
should burn in hell.

On August 28, 1862, there was
another battle at Bull Run, or Manassas
Junction, the same location as the battle
fought there last year. This time, however, it
involved many more men from both sides,
including our beloved 104th New York
Volunteers. The battle raged on for three
days. Once again, the Confederates were
victorious, and it looked like the rebel army
was getting closer and closer to Washington
and the northern states. There was great
concern that they would advance into Ohio
and Pennsylvania next. We anxiously
awaited word of any casualties incurred for
our local soldiers, but the news traveled
slowly. Unfortunately, thoughts and fears
do not move slowly, and they raced through
my young mind on a nightly basis. I prayed
for the safety of the Whitney boys and
James Luce. Hopefully, the war would end
soon, and they would return home
victorious. But I also sometimes wondered

what would happen if the rebels moved into New York and turned our tranquil Genesee Valley into a battlefield.

Less than three weeks after the smoke of muskets and cannons cleared over the fields of Bull Run, another attack and a subsequent battle occurred. This time, however, it was on Northern soil. Were my fears becoming a reality? Was this some sort of self-fulfilling prophecy?

I anxiously watched the newspaper for an accurate and conclusive account of the conflict. It came in late September when it was reported that on the seventeenth, Union forces attacked the Confederate army which had advanced into Maryland. This battle took place at Antietam Creek, near the town of Sharpsburg, Maryland.

Once again, the men of the 104th New York Infantry were involved in the fighting. Although the results of the battle were inconclusive, the rebel troops were the first to retreat back to Virginia, and the Union army claimed victory despite having almost 25 percent of their men either killed, wounded, or captured.

When considering both armies, nearly twenty-three thousand American men from both armies lost their lives in a single day of fighting. Among those was my friend Private Isaac Whitney.

He was fatally shot on the first day of the battle.

Dead at nineteen in a field in Maryland. The war had now touched my young life on a personal level.

CHAPTER 8

The War Drags On

There was still a need for more men to enlist in the Union army. Local officials were informed that if there weren't enough recruits, the government would institute a conscription to fill the ranks. Any town that failed to meet their quota of new recruits would be forced to implement a draft.

To house and train these additional troops, a new camp would have to be built. This time, however, it was constructed in the town of Portage, about twenty miles southwest of Geneseo. I thought what a shame and apparent waste it was that Camp Union had just been torn down. But by the fall of 1862, the new camp was complete and had a full contingent of new recruits. These troops received some hasty preliminary training and soon departed for Washington.

With the ongoing depletion of men from the ranks of our army and the continuation of fighting in the southern states, it appeared that a draft would be necessary in Geneseo. The deaths and causalities continued to mount, and our troops needed reinforcements if we were to win the war. The proposed draft would include all able-bodied male citizens between the ages of twenty and forty-five, except those who were physically or mentally unfit. Other exemptions would include the only son of a widow or infirm parents, the only brother of orphaned children under the age of twelve, the father of motherless children under the age of twelve, and anyone convicted of a felony.

Fortunately, my older brother Michael was only fourteen, and we didn't need to worry about him being drafted. And surely, the war could not continue another six years. My father was still legally eligible, but the thought of him being drafted at thirty-eight and with eight dependent children was unimaginable.

President Lincoln declared that Thursday, April 30, 1863, should be a day of fasting and prayer on behalf of the nation. He recommended that all businesses be closed as well. The vast majority of people in Geneseo took this to heart, and the streets of the village that afternoon appeared as if it were a Sunday. To emphasize that appearance, each of the churches held services. Our family observed the proposal; Father stayed home from work, and we all attended mass at Saint Mary's to pray.

Yet the war continued.

On into June, we received reports every week of many more men who were killed, wounded, or missing from the battlefields in the South. It appeared more and more likely that another draft would be necessary within the state in the near future.

Around this time, my father started hearing about a new movement underway involving a group of like-minded Irish Catholics that strongly opposed the war. They also opposed the draft, to the extent that they would resist, even to the point of armed conflict if necessary. The objective was to force an immediate peace settlement with the Confederates.

The Republicans started calling these anti-war Democrats "Copperheads." I guess they considered them poisonous snakes.

But Father, and most of his friends, primarily the Irish immigrants, felt inclined to support this growing cause. The Copperhead groups in the large cities, like New York and Boston, were much better organized, more vocal, and more likely to actually riot against the continued draft. In a small, mostly rural environment like Geneseo, any organization kept a much lower profile. The Irish immigrants generally felt like outcasts as it was; they didn't need to intensify that alienation in such a predominantly Republican town. But the anti-war sentiment was growing stronger with every new report of lost battles and lost lives and no end in sight.

Once again, General Robert E. Lee and the rebel army attempted to invade the North. Under the command of George Meade, our troops collided with Lee's near the small town of Gettysburg, Pennsylvania, on July 1, 1863. The fighting raged on for another two days, culminating in one last massive charge by the rebel army.

That final charge proved unsuccessful, and they were turned back, retreating into Virginia. The three-day battle resulted in the largest number of casualties of the entire war to date. The 104th New York Infantry was involved in a good part of the fighting and sustained many casualties. Nearly a quarter of the Union army were either killed, wounded, captured, or missing, and almost a third of the Confederate army met the same fate.

Of course, I didn't learn this news immediately. It took several days for the account to reach Geneseo and nearly a week more to print the particulars in the newspaper. This was my primary source of knowledge. I was an avid reader, even at the age of eleven, especially when it came to current events such as this.

Since I knew the 104th New York Infantry had been involved, and the casualty rate had been so high, I visited Margaret McLeod as soon as I was aware of the battle to see if she had received a letter from James Luce, her beau. She hadn't heard anything from him in nearly a month, and we both became quite concerned and prayed that he was not among the killed or wounded. Our fears subsided within a week when she finally received a letter from him after the battle. Hopefully, a guardian angel would watch over him for the duration of the war, and he would return to Geneseo, and Margaret unscathed.

Not all the causalities were on the field at Gettysburg that week.

On July 3, Mrs. McBride, our neighbor down the street, was accidentally shot in the neck by two men quarreling over a pistol. Harry Gummer and John Levy had been arguing as to who the gun's lawful owner was, and they began tussling. The gun discharged while in Mr. Gummer's possession, with the errant ball hitting poor Mrs. McBride. Fortunately, she survived the incident, and both men were arrested and put in jail.

This odd occurrence reinforced my belief in fate and destiny. Those two men could have just as easily been in front of our house, and it could have been Mama who was shot, perhaps fatally. Or one of us children shot out of a cherry tree. But for some reason, it was Mrs. McBride who just happened to be in that exact spot at that exact time. I believed that the course of our lives must adhere to some preconceived plan, divine or not, that we have little control over. Like a log, floating in the river, it goes where the river takes it.

As expected, a draft had been implemented in our town. Too many men had been injured and killed. The names of those required to report had been selected. We were all saddened to see the impact it had on some of the families. In one family with four boys eligible, three of them were drafted. In another family, where five Negro boys were eligible, four of them were taken. All three of the jewelers in the village were called to serve.

Fortunately, Father's name was not included.

It was possible, however, to avoid going off to war. Several local men who had been drafted were able to secure substitutes to serve for them. These surrogates charged upwards of $325 to serve the three-year term required. It was a lucrative business for the stand-ins, mostly single men that had thus far avoided selection, but a hefty price to pay for the draftees to get out of serving. Had Father been selected, or even Michael, if he was old enough, I doubt they would've paid someone else to represent them. They both had enough patriotic pride that they would serve if called, yet still remained opposed to the war and the subsequent conscription.

Once again, there was rumbling and a renewed sentiment among the Copperheads of the town. Not only did they want the draft abolished—and the war brought to a quick conclusion, even if it meant capitulation to the Confederate states—but they were appalled by the inequity of the selection process.

By early October, the draft requirements for New York State had been filled. At least there would be no more draftees called to war. But the war dragged on. So many young men and boys had boarded the train and left this town only to return in a casket or on crutches with baggy, flapping pant legs or sleeves. Their faces were never the same, and they all shared a hollow, empty look in their eyes. Hopefully, James Luce would return as the handsome, healthy man that had vowed to marry my friend Margaret McLeod.

We all needed a lighthearted diversion to take our minds off the war, and it came in the form of a traveling menagerie. The advertisement in the newspaper stated there would be an exhibit of six very rare and exotic animals passing through Geneseo on October 7. These creatures had just been imported into our country and were on their way to Cleveland to be added to Van

Amburgh's Mammoth Menagerie.
According to the newspaper ad, the six
included the only living giraffe on this
continent, a South American tapir, the only
living royal Bengal tiger in America, the
only black African ostrich ever imported,
the only living Poonah bear in America, and
the only living kangaroo in the country as
well. They had never been exhibited in
public, but two showings would be at the
fairgrounds that day. Father thought the
four of us older girls should witness these
creatures and gave us each fifty cents, half
to cover admission and the other half to
spend on ourselves. Mother stayed home
with the twins and young John, while Mary,
Catherine, Elizabeth, and I headed off to the
fairgrounds. Some of these animals I had
never even seen pictures of. It was thrilling
to stand so close to them. I never imagined
that I'd be standing only a few feet away
from a real tiger and staring into its eyes.
Our excitement lasted into the night, and it
was difficult to fall asleep after observing
such a group of rare and exotic creatures.

One evening the following week,
after we had cleaned up the dinner dishes,
Father remained in the kitchen, telling
Mama about the death of John Bogy. I sat
and listened attentively since this was my

friend Catherine Bogy's father. She hadn't had a good life since her mother drowned in the river last summer. Her father continued drinking and was gone from home for long periods of time. Actually, Catherine preferred it that way since when he was home, he'd usually get upset and beat her and her brothers over the smallest things. She lived with her two older brothers, James and John Jr.

Father recognized that the cause of his death was no surprise to anyone who knew him. He read aloud from the account in the *Livingston Republican*, "It's been some three months since John Bogy of this village enlisted in a regiment organized at Rochester, but was rejected. While in the city, he was sent to the workhouse for intemperance. His term expired on Thursday, and stopping at a drinking house, he obtained a bottle of liquor from which he drank to excess and died on Friday night. It will be recollected his wife drowned herself in the river a year or two ago."

Father added that there was now one less stereotypical drunken Irish bum in the town. His children would, sadly, be better off as orphans.

On Monday morning, the ninth of May 1864, rumors began swirling through the village like spring floodwater across the flats. Word had been received that General Wadsworth was wounded during a battle in Virginia sometime over the weekend. Additional rumors indicated that he had been captured and taken prisoner and may or may not have been wounded. As the stories circulated, the anxiety level rose when no official word came from the front lines. By late afternoon, speculation was put to rest when it was confirmed that the General had, indeed, been mortally wounded three days earlier. He had been shot in the forehead and died instantly.

Weeks later, we learned the real truth from an official report. He was shot in the back of his head on a Friday, fell from his horse, and was captured by Confederate forces pursuing his retreating troops. He died two days later in a Confederate field hospital.

All the bells in the village rang that Monday evening, and citizens were invited to gather at the American Hotel on Main Street, where the official announcement was made of this sad news. He was killed in Spotsylvania County, Virginia, during a battle that became known as the Battle of the Wilderness.

General James Samuel Wadsworth was born in Geneseo in 1807 and was fifty-seven at the time of his death. He was the oldest, and at the time, the only surviving child of the late James Wadsworth, founder of the town. Out of respect for the general, the Confederates allowed his son-in-law, Montgomery Ritchie, to retrieve the body from their field hospital to be sent home. It was announced that the body was expected to arrive in Geneseo on May 12 or 13 and that a funeral service would take place at Saint Michael's Episcopal Church the day after it arrived. Burial would be in the family plot at Temple Hill Cemetery.

Despite the many Union victories, there was no indication that the war was subsiding. We all feared that it would go on for years to come. Late in May, agents set up at the American Hotel to purchase horses from those able to sell. Over a thousand horses were needed to replenish the cavalry mounts that had been lost. Men were not the only ones to succumb to the ravages of war.

CHAPTER 9

Mixed Emotions

On Saturday, May 21, 1864, several young men from the village met at the American Hotel to organize a base ball club[3]. This sport was growing in popularity, and it was decided that Geneseo should form as many teams as possible to compete against other towns. By unanimous vote, it was determined that the name of the first team formed would be The Wadsworth Base Ball Club.

The first practice was held the following Saturday. There were base ball fields already at the Livingston County fairgrounds, just out Avon Street at the bottom of North Street. The fairgrounds had been permanently established at this

---

[3] As with the term "pic nic," this is how the original sport was spelled during the late nineteenth century.

location in 1849 on eight acres of land donated to the county by James Wadsworth. Six years later, the fairground area was expanded to about fourteen acres. Benches were now added at each playing field, on which spectators could watch and cheer the local team. Games were played every day of the week except Sunday.

My older sisters, Mary and Catherine, loved watching the games and the excitement of competition with neighboring towns. They took me along whenever they went. It was a pleasant diversion and helped take our minds off the continuing war. But the experience was short-lived, lasting an afternoon at best, and then I would be brought abruptly back to the reality of what was going on in the southern states. Reading the newspaper accounts and listening to discussions my father would have with other adults would bring it all back into focus. Even my afternoon porch discussions with Mr. Whitney would eventually get around to the war, recent battles, and his thoughts on what the government was doing right or doing wrong. My friend Margaret would usually join us on the porch, serving lemonade and sharing information she had received from James Luce.

On a late August afternoon of that year (1864), I found Margaret sobbing on the porch. She had just received a letter, not from James but from one of his friends in the same regiment. He wrote that James had given him her address and instructions to send a note should something happen to him. She dreaded reading any further. But she continued on, reading each word slowly, almost afraid to read the next one. The note went on to say that the 104th Infantry had been involved in a battle on August 18, just south of Petersburg, Virginia. It was being called the Battle of Globe Tavern. Although the Union army claimed a victory, over 250 men from their ranks were killed and more than 1,000 wounded. In addition, there were nearly three thousand soldiers captured, including most of Company D. She read on, squinting through tears, to learn that James had been among those captured.

Both Mr. Whitney and I tried to comfort her by stating the obvious, that at least he wasn't killed or maimed. And if there was a quick end to the war, he would return home to Geneseo and to her. Margaret resigned herself to the fact that she probably would not receive any letters from James himself, now that he was a prisoner of war.

Prayers were needed now more than ever that the war would end soon and that all of the troops would be delivered home safely, including all prisoners.

Yet, as feared, it was announced that more men would be needed for the Union army and navy. Geneseo's quota would be seventy men. At the time, there were about three hundred eligible if the draft were reinstated. Michael was now sixteen, and what had once seemed like an impossibility was suddenly becoming too close to reality. Thinking back to the death of Isaac Whitney, and now this recent news of James Luce, I feared what might become of my own brother should he be drafted.

We all expected the quota would be met with volunteers, but it seemed no one was stepping forward to enlist. The likelihood of another draft appeared to be imminent. By mid-September, the town's quota had been reduced to fifty-seven men, and fortunately, there were enough men and boys who ultimately volunteered, thereby preventing a draft. After the fall of Atlanta in September of 1864, a Union victory seemed within reach. Perhaps coincidentally, it also appeared as though the Copperhead movement had dwindled in support to almost nonexistence.

Hopefully, the war was in its final stages.

President Lincoln selected the last Thursday of November as a day of thanksgiving and prayer for the success the Union forces had had recently, as well as a rapid end to the war. In the future, this same day would be observed as a national day of thanksgiving, as a perpetual legacy, should he not be re-elected in the upcoming election. We all prayed that the war would end soon, and the troops on both sides would return home to their families and loved ones. I said an extra prayer for the safe return of James Luce to his bride-to-be.

The only disappointment on our first Thanksgiving Day dinner was that the rain hadn't let up. We'd had heavy rains for the entire month, and the streets and roads were almost impassable. The gravel that was applied to Center Street helped considerably, but it was less effective on other streets, especially the hills of North and South Streets. The streets that hadn't received a gravel topping, became a sea of mud and were very difficult to travel on.

Then, within a matter of days, the weather turned brisk and winter-like. The roads were essentially useless since that deep layer of mud had frozen into rigid ruts and were extremely difficult to navigate with a wagon, carriage, or sleigh. Only those who were forced to go out were seen on the streets, and then only in brief, scurrying flashes. I'd sit by the window within my warm house and watch to see if anyone was out and about. Over an hour had passed without sight of anyone.

The threat of a draft was as unrelenting as the snowfall. The first of January 1865 brought a new year, but the same persistent call for more enlistments. Another draft was scheduled for February 18. The quota for Geneseo was set at thirty-two men. Michael would turn seventeen this year, and my fear was that he would finally be called upon to fight. Why was this war dragging on so long? I didn't want my brother, father, or anyone else I knew drafted into the army.

The incentive for volunteers had increased to $300 for a one-year enlistment. A two-year enlistment was worth $400, and a three-year term was $500. I wondered if Michael would decide to enlist rather than wait for the draft. That was, after all, a lot of money. On the other hand, what good would it be if he was killed or captured in some battle? Despite the repeated victories of the Union army, the continuation of the draft and the monetary incentives were indications that the government was not as optimistic as I was that the war would end soon.

The supply of able-bodied men eligible for the draft seemed to have been exhausted. But there continued to be a good supply of "substitutes" who let it be known that should a draft be instituted, they would serve in place of anyone for the sum of $1,200, paid prior to leaving. Rumor had it that some of these substitutes would collect their fees, head off with the troops, and then desert as soon as they had the opportunity. Easy money if you didn't mind living on the run. I suppose that was a third option open to my brother. Not only could I not envision Michael as a soldier, but it was also inconceivable to imagine him a fugitive. On the other hand, there were many men who had no problem living outside the law.

Early in 1865, there was an attempted escape from the jail by two of its prisoners. One of them was a murderer. Fortunately, the escape attempt was caught in time, and they did not get away. But it did get the attention of the townspeople and the village board. For years, there had been complaints that the jail was not very secure. There were repeated attempts to escape each and every year. Part of the problem was that it was an old wooden structure, and there was significant rot in the floors and walls of some of the cells. Many people, not the least of whom the sheriff, felt that something should be done to improve the security of the cells or a successful escape would be inevitable.

Father heard from Mr. Whitney that James Luce had been reported dead. He shared what details he was aware of surrounding his death. I couldn't imagine the heartache that Margaret would be going through, and I knew she'd be inconsolable. I decided to give her some time to grieve, but I also wanted to be by her side. We had grown very close, and I knew how much she loved James. Her dream had been to spend the rest of her life with him and raise a family. And the feeling had been mutual. James had even listed her as his next of kin when he enlisted. She received the details of his passing via official government notice. He and his fellow prisoners had been sent to Salisbury Prison in North Carolina. Suddenly, this seemed so very far away.

Margaret shared the note with me several weeks later. It merely stated that James had died of disease while at the prison on February 14, 1865.

Valentine's Day.

The sad irony of it made my heart ache for Margaret.

I later learned, from reading at the library, just how horrible Salisbury Prison was, although I never shared this information with Margaret. It was the only wartime prison in North Carolina and was originally designed to hold about 2,500 soldiers. By the time James was taken there, the prisoner population was around ten thousand. Poor sanitation and overcrowding lead to a death rate of over 25 percent. It must have been like hell on earth for the poor souls taken there.

What a horrible way to die. Something no innocent person should have to endure. And to make the situation worse, his body would not be returned home. James, along with hundreds of other Union soldiers who died there, would be buried in a mass grave outside the prison walls. Poor Margaret would never even be able to visit his grave.

By the first week of March in 1865, the weather had turned springlike. Most of the snow had melted, and it began to rain. It rained for nearly a week. By March 15, the river had overflowed its banks as it typically did this time of year. But the rain continued, and two days later, the river had reached the highest point that most folks could remember. Once again, the valley took on the appearance of a vast lake, and we all headed down the hill to see the extent of it. I couldn't even tell where the river flowed beneath the surface. Farmers later reported that about two-thirds of the fences had been carried away. Over one hundred sheep and several head of cattle were swept away or drowned. All of the bridges north of Mount Morris were destroyed or severely damaged once again. The railroad and telegraph lines were out of commission, and there was no communication with the outside world for nearly a week.

The devastation downstream, in Rochester, was worse.

The most severe flood in the history of Geneseo hit Rochester with even greater brutality. The deluge caught the people in the city by surprise. Rochesterians were used to hearing reports of spring floods on the upper Genesee River and paid them little mind. Therefore, residents were not too concerned when news arrived of an abrupt March thaw and a drenching spring rain to the south. Ice jams and floating debris had begun blocking portions of the river near Avon, while the streams and creeks continued dumping thousands of gallons into it. Eventually, these unintentional dams broke open, and the tidal waves rushed toward Rochester with devastating fierceness.

When the floodwaters reached the city on Friday morning, March 17, the surge overflowed into the lumberyards above Court Street. Now with massive amounts of floating debris riding the rushing river, the arches beneath the bridges began to clog. The water, rising at a rate of ten inches an hour, soon spilled over the top of the aqueduct near Main Street, as if it were a dam. And when that last stronghold broke, the New York Central Railroad bridge was swept away. Along with several streetcars, the bridge went crashing over the brink of the High Falls, a few hundred yards downstream.

The rushing torrent also filled the arches of the Main Street bridge. Blocked by the buildings lining its north side, floodwaters coursed westward into Buffalo,

Front, Aqueduct, Mill, and State Streets. Soon the central part of the city was inundated. The water was six feet deep at the main intersection, the Four Corners, on that dreary Saint Patrick's Day. The only downtown traffic during the next two days was by rowboat. Lumber from the mill yards continued floating through the streets, crashing into buildings and causing many of them to collapse.

The flooded city was in near-total darkness that night because the gas plant was also submerged. When the new day's light had shown, 90 percent of the First Ward was underwater. By the end of the second day, most of the Second and Third Wards were submerged as well.

Although damage was estimated at a million dollars, miraculously, not one human life was lost.

Back in Geneseo, the following week, we learned that the Union army had been successful, after a long siege, in capturing Petersburg, Virginia. This city was key to the defense of Richmond, the capital of the Confederate States, and crucial for keeping supply lines open. Now that it was in the hands of Union troops, it seemed reasonable that the war would soon be over.

By the beginning of April, Richmond was abandoned, and the war seemed to be in its final days. The city was considered so secure, in fact, that President Lincoln toured the fallen city on April 4.

On April 9, 1865, ninety miles to the west of Richmond, the men of the 104th New York were engaged in the Battle of Appomattox Court House. They contributed to another decisive Union victory. This final defeat forced General Robert E. Lee to surrender the Confederate army that same afternoon.

The signing of the surrender had finally brought an end to the longest, costliest war the nation had ever seen.

What a wonderful present for my soon-to-be thirteenth birthday.

The people of Geneseo filled the streets when the news reached us. There were flags everywhere. The town band played all day and into the night. There were several large bonfires that night, and the townspeople stayed out, reveling, until well after midnight.

The celebration was short-lived, however. Just days after receiving this good news, we learned that President Lincoln had been assassinated.

On the night of April 14, Good Friday, he attended the theater with his wife in Washington. An assassin shot him in the back of the head shortly after ten, and he died about nine hours later.

The country had just been through four years of war, and now it was without its leader. A nation that should have been rejoicing began a period of grieving.

CHAPTER 10

Our Family Grows

Although the weather had its ups and downs, and the nation's emotions swung from high to low, the headcount within our little house on North Street was ever-increasing. On May Day in 1865, Mother gave birth to a baby girl. She would be the ninth and final child for my mother and father, who were now forty-two and forty-five, respectively. They named her Emma. Being thirteen myself, I was able to help much more around the house than I had during previous births. And Mama needed considerable help. The delivery had not been easy for her.

My oldest brother, Michael, now eighteen, had moved out of the house to live on a farm near Avon, where he worked as a hired hand. My sister Mary was sixteen and shared a bedroom with Catherine, Elizabeth, and me. My brother John, who was six, shared a bedroom with the twins, Anna and Ellen. The new baby slept in my parents' room.

I remember being intrigued by how our clothing styles varied dependent upon our age. Of course, infants were dressed in flowing gowns, as baby Emma was, but John had only recently been dressing in typical boy's clothing. As for my sisters and me, the length of our skirts was a reflection of our age. As girls got older, they wore longer skirts. The twins, who were seven, wore skirts slightly above their knees. Elizabeth and I had skirts that came right to our knees. Catherine's dresses fell below her knees, almost to mid-calf, and Mary's dress was just above her ankles.

Most boys would probably hate living in a house with seven sisters, but John was very protective of us all and helped Mama a lot since he was the "man of the house" while Father was working. The only thing he was barred from doing was filling the lamps with kerosene oil or lighting them, tending to the stove, or anything else that involved fire or hot metal parts. Father, being deathly afraid of fire starting in the house, took extreme precautions with all of our lamps and tallow candles, as well as the ash bin for the stove. He made sure we had a good fire in the stove before leaving for work and was usually home before lamps needed to be lit. His rule was that only in a dire emergency should anyone else deal with these sources of combustion. We wisely followed his orders.

During the summer of '65, several of our neighbors became quite bewildered by the sudden loss of fruit from their backyard orchards. Both Catherine Houston's and Miranda Davis's peach and pear trees had succumbed to this mysterious phenomenon. Just as the fruit was ripening and the trees were about to offer a worthwhile harvest, owners would awaken to find them almost bare. This was happening all around town and was initially thought to be the work of birds or some other pest. Eventually, several boys were caught red-handed, stealing at night, and admitted that it had become somewhat of a sport or challenge. They called it "cooning" and there were quite a few young men engaged in it. On September 15, three boys were caught in the act and immediately arrested for it. Suddenly the trees seemed to have much more fruit available for harvest, and I knew we'd have peaches and pears available to preserve for the winter. It also wasn't uncommon for Miranda and me to pick a bushel or two of fruit and sell it to Birge's Grocery House on Main Street. We'd split the money between us and buy treats for ourselves or small gifts for our families. We only picked from trees on our own properties, so we weren't breaking the law, and it provided us with a little spending money throughout the summer. We'd pick cherries in July and peaches and pears in August. Apples usually weren't ready until September, and by that time, we were back in school, and our days as "fruit farmers" had drawn to a close. But the taste sensation of biting into a fully ripe peach or pear, sitting beneath the tree that produced it, is an experience that lasts forever.

On October 18, 1865, a plot to murder Sheriff Chase's son, Charles, was discovered and fortunately thwarted. At the time, there were fourteen prisoners confined in the jail, including one woman. Each of them was being held on crimes that would ultimately send them to the state prison in Auburn. Sheriff Chase was away on business, and Charles was acting as the jailor while he was gone. Nine of the prisoners had concocted a plan to escape during the sheriff's absence. Their scheme was to murder Charles when he came in to lock them up for the night. They would then take his body to the door that led to the outside, in which there was a hole he had to put his hand through since this portion of the building was locked from the outside. His mother would recognize his hand from the ring on his finger and would open the door. They'd then rush out, bind and gag all the women in the house, and make their escape.

Fortunately, the sheriff returned early and spoiled their plan after two of the prisoners alerted him to the scheme.

The ringleader was a fellow by the name of Henry Wilson, who was in jail under indictment for the murder of Henry DeVoe from the town of Portage. His trial began the week after this failed escape, and he was convicted and sentenced to be hanged on the twenty-second of December. Father would never allow any of us to attend a public execution, but I must admit my curiosity was difficult to contain. Secretly, I couldn't wait to read about the affair in the paper on Friday morning.

The execution was carried out right on the courthouse lawn. As I carefully read the account in the *Livingston Republican*, I could almost feel myself among the crowd of spectators huddled together on that cold

December morning. I continued reading, oblivious to my actual surroundings.

Standing on the scaffold, Wilson was asked if he had any last words. After rambling for about ten minutes, he became quiet. The noose was put around his neck and a black cap placed over his head. His lawyer bid him good-bye, and the sheriff told him he had four minutes to live.

Wilson replied, "It is not much consolation to be kept standing here in the cold three or four minutes. I might as well go now as any time."

To that, the sheriff replied, "Very well, if that is your desire." The cap was drawn over his face, and the sheriff added, "Wilson, your time is up."

He replied, "Go ahead," and the weight was dropped.

The spring of 1866 was uneventful, aside from my turning fourteen. My sister Catherine was still at home, but now both Mary and Michael had moved out. This created more room in our house, but also more responsibility. Mother had become ill during the winter and spent several weeks bedridden. Catherine and I were able to take care of the children. Taking care of little John and the twins, who were now eight years old, and baby sister Emma, took a considerable amount of time and effort. Keeping them fed and in clean clothing was a full-time job. We tried to maintain the same schedule as Mother, and I gained an appreciation for just how hard it was to simply provide clean laundry for our family.

Mondays were always "wash day" in our house, as well as most other families. But properly doing the laundry took considerably more than one day. Catherine and I at least had a good supply of soap on hand, and the cistern provided an ample amount of rainwater, so we had all the materials we needed.

Our routine consisted of sorting all the clothing and linens on Saturday and mending anything that needed it. On Sunday, we would soak everything in warm water with a few soap flakes shaved off the bar and some washing soda or lye. We'd add a bit of Mrs. Stewart's Bluing to the whites if they appeared dingy or yellowish. Early Monday morning, with a nice fire going in the stove, we'd begin heating water in the big copper washtub. We'd also fill a couple of wooden tubs with water from the cistern.

Father made sure the fire was adequate before he left for work. The actual washing process consisted of four steps. First, we'd rub the clothes with soap against the washer board until a good lather was achieved. Then they were wrung out. Next, the clothing was turned inside out and using fresh water, the process of soaping, rubbing, and wringing was repeated. Following that, items were boiled in soapy water for several minutes and then retrieved using our long sticks. When cool enough to handle, we'd wring them out again and rinse everything thoroughly in fresh, clean water. One last wringing out, and everything was hung up to dry.

If the weather was warm and not raining, we'd hang the items on our clothesline in the backyard and drape them over the bushes if we ran out of room. Sometimes, we'd just lay wet sheets on the lawn to dry in the sun. If it was raining or too cold, we'd use the indoor drying rack, but it would fill up fast, and we'd resort to simply hanging wet laundry anywhere we could around the house.

After the laundry was dry, it needed to be starched and ironed on Tuesday. This was a miserable, hot, dangerous chore that required another full day. Once again,

Father would make sure we had a nice fire in the stove early in the morning to keep the flat irons, placed on top, hot enough to do their job. I trusted Catherine to handle most of this work, but since it was strenuous, I'd relieve her from time to time. These smoothing irons, or sad irons, weighed almost ten pounds apiece. Two were required: one to be heating up on the stove while the other was being used and therefore cooling down. These irons got very hot and had to be held with a thick rag around the handle. The bottom of the irons needed to be kept scrupulously clean so as not to stick and scorch the linens. A quick wipe with a little beeswax helped prevent sticking to heavily starched fabrics. Achieving just the right temperature was a fine art, but I remembered my mother's technique for determining when an iron was ready but not so hot that it would scorch. She'd spit on the iron's flat surface and observe how quickly and vigorously the moisture dissipated. I mastered the technique quicker than Catherine did, and she relied on me to keep her supplied with an efficient iron during the day.

Our washing process involved only body linen, underclothing, and household linens like sheets, towels, and kitchen cloths. Our outer clothing was usually just brushed clean. But being a family of nine, it took a considerable amount of time as it was. It seemed like we'd just get the finished items put away when we'd have to start the sorting process all over again.

My schoolwork suffered during the weeks Mother was ill, and I knew I was slipping behind my friends. I was unable to attend school every day and had no time to study at home. But I felt an obligation to my mother and family. I knew how hard Father worked to earn money for the family, and I wanted to contribute as much as I could.

By early summer, Mother seemed her old self again, and there were no lingering effects from the illness that kept her down during the winter. Now that school was out for the summer, what extra time I could have had for myself, I devoted to helping Mama as much as I could in taking care of our family. I learned a lot from her that summer with respect to keeping a home, and I recognized that someday I'd need those skills for maintaining my own house and family.

On the morning of the Fourth of July, I woke to the sound of rain hitting my bedroom window. Not only was it raining hard, but the wind was blowing, and it appeared that the festivities planned for our Independence Day would be as damp as the sidewalks and street outside our house. By noon, however, the sun had come out, the wind had calmed down, and the celebration went ahead as planned.

There was quite a parade down Main Street, consisting of three fire companies and two martial bands as well as a swarm of young children on scooters and bicycles. Flags and banners were everywhere. The red, white, and blue buntings decked out on the Main Street hotels stirred up an emotional and patriotic feeling in everyone, especially after having just experienced the horrors of war. There were speeches from the porch of the Eagle Hotel throughout the afternoon. The parade participants marched the length of Main Street, from the village park all the way to the fairgrounds.

My entire family watched the parade from makeshift benches along Main Street, then walked to the fairgrounds to observe the horse fair that was going on there. After some time taking in all there was to see, we headed up North Street and home to rest for the evening ahead. Shortly after dinner, another parade of the fire companies and bands marched the reverse direction, back down Main Street, from the fairgrounds to the park.

As the sun set over the far side of the valley, we gathered in the park and watched the darkening sky light up with a grand display of pyrotechnics.

What started out as a day with thunder and pouring rain ended with the explosive booms and the falling twinkles of fireworks.

The walk home seemed like another, smaller parade all by itself. The fire brigades and bands had been replaced by neighbors, the songs of children, and slightly inebriated men.

It was around this time, the summer of 1867, that I truly began to appreciate the village I lived in. It had all the conveniences of a larger city like Rochester but felt more intimate, friendlier, and was easier to get around in. All of the streets in the village were in very good condition, and there were new sidewalks installed on each of them. There was a wide variety of stores along Main Street, and there was nothing imaginable that couldn't be bought in one of them. You could walk from any location in the village to any other, at any time of the day or night, both easily and safely.

There was a newly constructed Episcopal church on Main Street, which was considered to be one of the finest in the state. In addition, there was a Methodist church and two Presbyterian churches, plus our own Catholic church right down the street. There was both a public and a private school. There was a free public library with over seven thousand volumes, I'm told. There were two large reading rooms available to the public that received one hundred different newspapers and publications, twenty of which were received on a daily basis. There was no excuse for anyone to be unaware of current events, locally, nationally, or worldwide.

There were fine hotels and boarding houses, two livery stables and, of course, our own train terminal. Our village, and most of the citizens in it, was certainly something to be proud of. As I turned fifteen that year, I realized just how fortunate I was and became very appreciative of all that was provided me, and that my family had been spared any personal tragedy.

CHAPTER 11

Base Ball and Sam Carey

As I became a little older and more independent, I found that I thoroughly enjoyed watching the relatively new game of base ball. My sister Catherine, Miranda Davis, Josephine Hull, and I spent many summer days at the fairgrounds where the games were played. One of our favorite teams to watch was the Geneseo Livingstons. They were quite talented and had won twelve out of sixteen games by midsummer.

An even more prominent club from town was the Hunkidory. They were undefeated in games against all of the Western New York teams and had to play teams from out of state to find more challenging opponents.

It was at a game being played between the Hunkidory and a team from Canada that I first laid eyes on Samuel Carey, although I didn't know his name at the time.

He was ruggedly handsome, with wavy dark hair and eyes as green as the fields of his homeland. He was seated with several other men, on the same set of benches as me. I found myself glancing over at him more often than I was watching the game. I almost couldn't take my eyes off him. I noticed that he was cheering for the same plays and the same team I was. At least we had that in common, right off the bat.

I was fifteen years old, and I believed I was falling in love. It was a unique, somewhat odd feeling I had never experienced before. But when compared to the emotions that Margaret McLeod had shared with me about James Luce, I thought it must be love.

Unfortunately, the summer was drawing to a close, and I knew I'd soon be back in school and wouldn't have time to attend many more games. I talked Catherine, and either Miranda or Josephine, into going to every game we could for the remainder of the summer in hopes of seeing the handsome stranger. I'm sure they suspected my interest in base ball neatly coincided with the attraction to the same group of men present at almost every game. After a little detective work, I learned that the object of my interest was named Samuel Carey.

Each time I saw him, he grew more and more handsome, and I'd often find my heart racing as I watched him from the security of my spot among friends. I hoped he'd notice me, at least once, but I was also terrified as to how I'd react if he actually did. I knew if I told Catherine of my true feelings, she'd probably go right up and share that information with him. For that reason alone, I tried to hide my feelings for him as much as I could from my sister. I also didn't want him to know that I was smitten.

School began, and I needed to refocus my mind on making sure I attended as many days as I could. I studied hard in hopes of catching up a bit from what I had missed in the spring.

Although I hadn't seen Sam Carey since the first week of September, I had difficulty getting him out of my mind. Many days in school, my thoughts would drift back to one of those base ball games, and I found it difficult to concentrate on my schoolwork. It was too easy to picture him standing and cheering some great play on the field or simply joking and laughing with his friends.

At home, it was easier; there were enough distractions and things that needed doing that I rarely thought about him. The only time I'd envision him, or hear his laugh, was while I was lying in bed, just about to drift off to sleep. I even found myself dreaming about him. Yet I also realized I didn't know much about this man who frequented my nocturnal dreams as often as my daytime thoughts. I barely knew his name and that he was Irish. I didn't know how old he was. I didn't even know where he lived. I didn't know where he worked or what he did to earn a living. And I didn't know how I was going to find out.

My sister Catherine recognized how obsessed I was becoming with this virtual stranger, and she would try to keep me grounded in reality. But she also realized that I was fifteen and becoming a young woman whose focus in life had changed from backyard cherry tree climbing to romance.

Kate

Mother Nature was keeping me grounded in reality, as well. The fall of 1867 was one of the driest I could remember. We had been experiencing a drought for several months. I quickly learned it can be just as devastating to have too little water as too much. Most of the wells and cisterns were very low or completely dry. What water there was became increasingly impure. Many typhoid fever cases were cropping up around town, which were being blamed on drinking this poor-quality water. My thoughts always drifted back to young Willie Lincoln and how his fate had been influenced by something we all needed to survive.

When both Catherine and Mother began showing symptoms of typhoid, the doctor was called, and he prescribed frequent doses of pure charcoal. I took responsibility for administering this "medicine" to both of them and provided frequent sponging to help with the fever. Preparing the charcoal remedy involved plucking a live coal from the fire, blowing off the ash, and then pulverizing it quickly in a mortar. Two to three teaspoons of this powder were then mixed with a little pure, clean water and swallowed. The doctor suggested that this concoction be taken every two hours while awake, and the illness should subside within two weeks. Fortunately, both Mother and Catherine survived and were much better in half that time.

On February 6 of 1868, the town experienced a horrific tragedy, one likely never to be forgotten by the few citizens who witnessed it. In the middle of that frosty night, the "crazy house" burned to the ground, with five female inmates locked inside.

The "crazy house" was a two-story wooden structure that sat behind the county home's main brick building. At three in the morning, several neighbors were awakened by screams from the inmates and an eerie orange glow in the sky. They immediately sent out an alarm and quickly joined other villagers rushing to the scene. But with no water available on the premises, they could not fight the fire, and the building was quickly destroyed. Every effort was made to rescue the building's inmates, but only eight of the thirteen occupants escaped alive. The others were slowly consumed by the flames. Those who rushed to help would never forget the nightmarish screams for the rest of their lives.

Only after the building had burned down completely were the five badly burned bodies retrieved from the ashes.

Coroner Chase held an inquest the following afternoon. John Stewart, who had charge of the building, testified that he was awakened around three o'clock by the screaming of the women and found the building already filled with smoke. He sprang out of bed and unlocked all of the cell doors so the women could escape. He pulled nine of the women from their cells. Eight of them ran from the building, but the ninth ran back into her cell, and she, along with four others, perished in the subsequent inferno.

Charles Hysler, a thirty-two-year-old German immigrant, was an inmate of the poorhouse and had worked in the washhouse for three years. The washhouse was actually just a room in the lower story of the crazy house where the laundry for the entire facility was done. He had charge of the two fireplaces in the washhouse, one for heating water and the other for heating the building. He started them each morning and extinguished them each evening, carrying the ashes outside in a metal bucket.

He claimed he put out the fire on Wednesday night before supper and locked up the washhouse. He was the only person with a key. One witness testified that she saw Laura Balcom go into the washhouse at about 8 p.m. Wednesday evening to meet Hysler, but he denied that allegation. Several other witnesses testified that Hysler and Laura were often caught together. Mr. Stewart confirmed that he had found them together on several occasions and considered it inappropriate. Miss Balcom, herself an inmate, was twenty-six years old.

Although the inquest was inconclusive about how the fire started, the rumor and public opinion was that Hysler and Laura Balcom went into the washhouse at 8 p.m., built a fire for their own use, and left it burning when they went out again later.

The women who died such a horrible death were Mary Lord, 50, born in Canada; Mary Bolton, 49, born in England; Sophia Sample, 64, born in the U.S.; Ann Coogan, 29, born in Ireland; and Emelline Wallace, 39, born in the U.S. All of these women were considered incurably insane, but they didn't deserve the manner in which they perished.

Growing up within a mile or so of this structure, it had always seemed a sinister and threatening place to us children. To our young eyes and imaginations, it could easily have been a haunted castle, complete with a dungeon. There were stories about what went on within its walls that would send chills down my spine. It was definitely off-limits to us children. Even the bravest boys wouldn't dare get close enough for a peek through the barred windows, but some came close enough to hear moans and screams coming from within its walls.

Among adult discussions, the facility went by various names, from the county home to the county poorhouse or almshouse, to the lunatic asylum, but all would agree that it was a rather dismal place to spend time in.

The large, main building was a three-story brick structure with two attached wings. The basements of each housed the male "lunatics," who were kept confined and separated from the female inmates.

A teacher was employed at the facility for nine or ten months a year to instruct the children. There was also a physician on the payroll who visited the facility whenever called. Limited facilities existed for bathing, and, in general, the sexes were not kept isolated. It was not uncommon for several of the female inmates to become pregnant at any given time. Those inmates deemed "hopeless lunatics" were confined, individually, to a single cell. This was the only means of restraint for most inmates; however, in extreme situations, handcuffs were employed to prevent harm to either themselves or the attendants.

The insane received no actual medical attention or treatment for their mental illness. Nor was the facility in the habit of providing a proper classification of the patients. The building housed not only the mentally ill but also those who had fallen on hard times. The vast majority, nearly three-quarters of the paupers housed there, were there due to their intemperate habits. The power of discharge was solely at the discretion of the superintendent.

Learning these things about the "poorhouse," as I called it, from a myriad of questions I continuously posed, gave me a greater appreciation for the things we had. My family lived in a happy, although crowded home, always had plenty to eat, and everyone was relatively healthy.

    The summer of '68 was another hot one. During the first two weeks of July, the daily temperature averaged ninety-eight degrees in the shade. Since there were no Fourth of July festivities in Geneseo that year, Catherine, Miranda, and I decided to travel to the Avon Driving Park, have a pic nic lunch, and watch the horse races. While there, I encountered my brother and a group of his friends. Unlike us, who were only spectators, they were placing bets on the outcome of each race. There were perhaps a dozen young men with Michael, and I noticed Sam Carey was among them. Sam and my older brother had apparently become friends, or at least they had friends in common. I saw this as a golden opportunity to finally meet the man I had been secretly dreaming about. I pointed this out to Catherine, and she giddily dared me to go over and talk to him. After mustering up enough courage, I walked over and introduced myself to Sam as Michael's kid sister. My heart was racing, but I wanted to prove to Catherine that I was a mature young woman who took the initiative of an introduction. I imagined it would probably impress Miranda as well. Sam smiled and told me he was very happy to meet me, and with that, I turned and sauntered back to my girlfriends with my heart still pounding.

When the last race ended, Michael, Sam, and their group headed for the train station for the ride home to Geneseo. I returned by buggy with Catherine and Miranda, not wanting to ride the train with a group of men. Michael, and I assume everyone else in that group, had been drinking most of the afternoon.

Shortly after the train departed for Geneseo, Michael noticed Miss Mary Dennis riding in the same car. The car was full of passengers, and since the ride was of relatively short duration, many of the travelers were standing in the aisles.

Mary was the daughter of John Dennis, a hardworking, well-respected Negro mason who lived on Temple Hill Street, not far from our house. John had several daughters, all rather attractive, but Mary was the youngest. She was seventeen at the time.

My brother, four years older and full of Avon whiskey, tried to embrace her, probably more to impress his friends than to satisfy any personal desires. As he tried to put his arms around her, she pushed back his advance. Evermore determined now, he attempted again, and this time, she dealt him a blow to the face with the handbag she was carrying.

She hit him so hard that he landed on the floor, and several people around him nearly lost their balance, too. He gathered himself up with a bruised ego and an aching jaw and stumbled back to his group.

After being taunted by his companions, he decided he wasn't about to let this young Negro girl get the best of him.

He slowly worked his way back to her, and despite the glaring look in her eyes, he once again attempted to embrace her. Before he even got his second hand on her, she dealt him another, more vicious blow with her handbag. Again, Michael ended up on the floor of the railroad car, this time with a bloodied nose. Seeing the blood from his nose and feeling the humiliation growing within him, he ripped off his coat and headed toward her with fire in his eyes.

Mary's brother, who had remained uninvolved since it had appeared she was handling the situation suitably, decided it was time to intervene.

He was a large man with the powerful arms and hands of a mason, just like his father. Before Michael was within arm's reach of her, he was pushed back into his group of friends who had gathered closer to see what would happen next. Soon, fists were flying as Michael's pals stepped in to confront the black man who was now shoving their friend. A real brawl ensued and raised such a commotion that the train was stopped, and Michael and his friends were put off. They ended that Fourth of July by having to walk back to Geneseo, arriving well after midnight, but more sober than when they left Avon.

I heard this story the following day and was told that although Sam Carey was in the same car, he did not get involved in the brawl. I felt relieved by this news since I knew my brother to be a hot-tempered Irishman, and I was hoping Sam Carey was different. In my mind, he was already my boyfriend, and if we were to become more serious, I'd want him to act more civil than my brother after he'd been drinking.

Sam Carey and I spent a substantial amount of time together that summer. We would attend every base ball game we could in Geneseo, and occasionally travel to Avon or Lima to watch our favorite sport.

Just the two of us.

How far our relationship had grown from only a year ago when I was too afraid to speak to him.

One day we walked all the way to Fall Brook, about two miles south of the village, to sit on the edge of the gorge and take in the splendor of the falls. Fall Creek, or Fall Brook, cascades about seventy feet into a narrow ravine before it winds its way into Little Beard's Creek further west, and subsequently into the Genesee River. Where the two creeks join was very near the site of the Boyd and Parker massacre that was after the American War of Independence.

But our thoughts were only for each other, the beautiful day, and the serenity of the cascading waters beside us. Summer evenings would often find us walking along Main Street, strolling in the park, or sitting by the train depot watching the sunset over the valley.

He loved to fish in the river at the foot of Court Street, and he taught me to fish as well. We'd sit for hours on the sunbaked rocks along the riverbank, not really caring if we caught fish or not. We were content just being together, listening to the birds singing in the treetops against the muddy river's whisper-like flow at our feet.

I had fallen in love with Sam Carey, and I truly believed that he was in love with me.

That summer, I realized he was the man I wanted to spend the rest of my life with. I was sixteen years old, and I knew plenty of girls who were married at that age. I also sensed that my father had serious doubts about Sam becoming an honorable husband. Perhaps we could prove him wrong. The fact that he was six years older than me and was an Episcopalian didn't help sway Father's opinion that he would make a suitable mate for any of his daughters.

Mama, on the other hand, was very tolerant and didn't discourage my relationship with him. She never let it show if she was opposed to my involvement with an older, non-Catholic man. I knew that she would wish us the best and be fully supportive of our future together.

Now I just needed Sam to come to the same realization and propose that we marry.

Samuel Carey didn't come to the United States until 1861 when he landed in Boston along with his older brothers at the age of fifteen. They all came from Tipperary in Ireland. While his brothers settled in Boston, young Sam ventured west to the fertile lands of the Genesee, having heard of the job opportunities here.

He was a country boy at heart and couldn't envision living in the city, any city, especially in a poor urban neighborhood packed with Irish immigrants. He witnessed the life his brothers were settling for— working the docks, living in a tenement slum, and spending most of their earnings on whiskey, women, and games of chance. Perhaps he was naïve, but Sam envisioned a better life for himself and headed west to cleaner air and a healthier lifestyle. He was searching for a land similar in nature to the Golden Vale he had left behind in County Tipperary. Fate brought him to Geneseo, and by 1864, he had taken up residence and was working as a day laborer in my town. He was living in a boarding house on Main Street—how our paths never crossed until three years later remains a mystery to me. But I believed it was destiny that brought us together, and we would eventually marry and raise a family in the town we both loved.

By July of 1868, all the mills from Mount Morris to Rochester suspended operations because of the low and stagnant river, and the intense heat. Sam and I went fishing one day, and it proved useless. I couldn't imagine any fish in the shallow, muddy water, so I convinced Sam to give up and walk with me to the fairgrounds where we could get a cold drink and rest in the shade.

Walking up the Court Street hill with the temperature above one hundred took all the strength I had, and it was such a relief to settle into the shade of a large oak tree. Sam fetched us a couple of ice-cold lemonades. As we relaxed and gazed at the high wispy clouds, he told me a circus was traveling through the county the following week, and he'd like to take me to it. Bryan's Grand Caravan, Menagerie, and Circus was to be in

Mount Morris on July 21. I told him I'd love to go with him and thanked him for asking.

Tuesday afternoon, we boarded the train, and in less than an hour, we were walking past a collection of rare birds and beasts, and into the circus tent to watch the performers.

Despite being dreadfully hot, we enjoyed ourselves and didn't take the train back to Geneseo until well after sundown. Sam walked me home from the depot to the top of North Street, holding my hand the entire way.

As we approached my house, he asked if I would marry him.

I felt my heart begin to race again, and I became a little light-headed and thought I might faint right there on the sidewalk.

It could have been the warm, humid air, or the nearly two-mile walk uphill from the depot, or simply the realization that my dream had come true, and I was about to become a real woman and a wife. More than likely, it was a combination of all three.

I told him I would love to marry him. I also let him know that he needn't go through the formality of asking my father's permission beforehand. I could see a sense of relief in his eyes. I assured him that I would inform my parents and gain their blessing.

I kept Sam's proposal a secret for several days. I'm not sure why I didn't share this news with anyone. Maybe I just wanted to gain some confidence before taking such a big step. Perhaps it was the uncertainty of how people would react. I expected my girlfriends to be thrilled, but I wasn't so sure about my parents.

I would lie awake at night, finding it difficult to fall asleep with so many thoughts swirling in my head. I tried to imagine my future as a wife and possibly a mother. Would I be happy in those roles?

After three days of harboring my secret, and as many nights of fitful sleep, there was a thunderstorm so severe it rattled our house as if it was being bombarded. Flashes of lightning lit up the night sky as if it were noon. The roar of thunder sounded as if the troops were back at Camp Union, engaged in an artillery drill. A lightning bolt struck a tree in Mr. Hooker's front yard, only a dozen houses away from us. We discovered the next morning that the bolt had split the tree in half, sending fragments of it flying hundreds of feet. Fifteen windows were shattered between his and the two neighboring houses.

Even closer to home, another lightning bolt struck an apple tree in Mr. Whitney's backyard. A large limb was ripped off the tree before the lightning continued on to hit his row of beehives. It completely shattered the first one in line, as if someone had placed a bomb inside it.

It was the very next morning when Father seemed to be in a rather sociable mood, that I told him Sam had proposed to me. I had informed my girlfriends the afternoon before and swore them to secrecy, and they faithfully agreed. Maybe it was being so close to the destruction of the thunderstorm the night before, but Father consented and gave me his blessing to begin a wedded life with Sam. Mother was thrilled, but my younger sisters and John seemed rather indifferent. Catherine was extremely excited about the news and assured me it was the best thing for me. Hopefully, that storm was not an omen of our future together, and our married life would be as pleasant as the sunny days of spring.

When I told Sam that we had my parents' blessing to marry, he said he'd like to take my entire family to Silver Lake for a day and have a pic nic lunch to celebrate.

Early Saturday morning, August 22, he pulled up in front of our house in a borrowed carriage, and we headed to Silver Lake. Although it was considerably farther away than Conesus Lake, our usual retreat, it felt both fascinating and fashionable to be traveling to this new destination. No one in my family had ever been, although we'd heard much about it. It was located near the village of Perry, in Wyoming County, about fifteen miles away. Given that we had a four-hour ride ahead of us, we departed shortly after the sun came up. Father was working that day, so Mother and I took all the younger children: Lizzie, John, Anna and Ellen, and baby Emma along with Sam. It was an ideal summer day with clear blue skies and plenty of sunshine, yet not unbearably hot. We arrived at the lake to find more than a hundred carriages parked around it. It seemed like everyone in the two-county area had the same idea for a day's enjoyment.

I had considered purchasing a bathing dress to bring with me and possibly taking a dip in the lake. But with concerns over the possible lack of changing facilities and not wanting to leave Lizzie and Mother responsible for watching the younger ones, I quickly abandoned that idea. The truth be told, I'd never been fond of going in the water and was just generating excuses.

A widely held medical opinion was that women should exercise and engage in mild recreation from a very early age. Although some experts warned that a woman's reproductive function might be compromised if the activities were too vigorous, it was generally agreed upon that women would be healthier if they participated in modest physical activities such as swimming. Furthermore, swimming was a valuable skill in the event of an accident during boating or other activities near water. Newspapers urged readers to learn to swim for self-protection, if for no other reason. During the "drowning season," stories of deaths and rescues were common. Having never spent time in any significant body of water, I didn't know if I could swim or not. I'd never tried.

Silver Lake had become famous for "sea serpent" sightings during the past decade. On the night of July 13, 1855, four men who were out fishing on the lake observed a giant (they estimated it to be sixty feet in length) serpent with glowing red eyes within five feet of the stern of their boat. Each of the men testified independently as to what they observed that evening, and there was little deviation in their statements. Needless to say, this created quite a frenzy in the area. Before long, more than one hundred additional people claimed to have seen the giant beast as well. The serpent was usually observed at night, and generally during inclement weather. But there was at least one occasion when it was spotted at noon on a clear, sunny day. There were no boats on the water at the time, but at least six independent witnesses observed it from the shore.

People were traveling from as far away as Europe to catch a glimpse of the creature.

One of the primary beneficiaries of this phenomenon was Artemus B. Walker, who owned the Walker House Hotel on Silver Lake. Business was booming with the influx of the curious, seeking to spot the legendary monster. However, his good fortune took a turn for the worse when, in 1857, a fire broke out in the hotel. Firefighters tried desperately to save the structure, but the inferno was intense, and the entire building burned to the ground. After the flames were extinguished and the smoldering rubble had cooled, they discovered something quite strange in the ruins.

They found the charred remains of a huge amount of greenish canvas entangled within a coiled wire frame and a giant pair of bellows.

Shortly after the fire and subsequent discovery, Walker left town in fear of the social consequences, both personally and professionally. He had returned just this summer (1868) and discovered that the townspeople now regarded him as somewhat of a hero. Perry and Silver Lake were doing a thriving business, and people were still skeptical as to whether or not a sea creature really existed.

Legend had it that sightings occurred well before Mr. Walker's hoax of 1855. In fact, an elderly American Indian who lived in the area claimed that Seneca and Mohawks would not camp by that particular lake because they had been frightened by a monster that lived within its waters.

Whether or not a creature lived in Silver Lake remained a mystery to us that day. There were no sightings from us, despite staring out over the lake from the shade of a large oak tree, for a good portion of the day. Our pic nic was most enjoyable, and Sam was very much a gentleman to Mother, me, and the children. We headed for home around three in the afternoon and were back by dusk.

I have to admit, that was one of the best days I had shared with Sam since I met him.

CHAPTER 12

Newlyweds

Since Sam and I had set our wedding date for November 22, 1868, I didn't return to school in September. Rather, I stayed home and assisted Mother as much as I could since she would soon be losing another teenage helper. Elizabeth, who was fifteen, would now be the oldest child in the house. She could help tend to the twins, young John and baby Emma, now three. It would still be a rather crowded house, but there would be one less mouth to feed.

On November 22, after the morning mass, Sam and I were married in Saint Mary's Catholic Church by Father Edward McGowan. Besides my parents, Michael and Mary were the only family in attendance. Michael, who had moved to Rochester, returned for the wedding. Both he and my sister Mary served as the official witnesses to our marriage vows.

I was pleased that several friends and neighbors could attend such a joyous occasion in my life. My friends Catherine Houston and Miranda Davis were delighted to come, and I was very surprised to see even Mr. Silas Whitney among the well-wishers after the service. Sam had a couple of his friends present, but no family members.

Sam had rented a small apartment on Main Street, and we spent the following week moving our worldly possessions into it and setting up our new home. That winter brought a new feeling of freedom and responsibility to me. Sam had become accustomed to living on his own, but this was a new undertaking for me. Although I was only sixteen, I was now the lady of the house, and with only slight assistance from my mother, began a very domesticated lifestyle. Of course, Mother had already taught me how to cook for a family, wash and mend clothing, and tend to all the other household chores, but now I was on my own to practice those skills.

Sam was pleased with how I ran the house, and he found jobs whenever and wherever he could. Unlike my father, who had a steady, almost guaranteed job as a farm laborer for the Wadsworths, Sam was more of a domestic laborer. He worked on the construction of new houses and buildings in Geneseo, as well as the occasional handyman work he could pick up when available. And rather than sit idle myself, I would take in clothing that needed mending and socks that needed darning from some of my more affluent neighbors on Main Street.

In the spring of 1869, I realized I was pregnant and that soon I would add motherhood to my new life. The year progressed with the usual annual occurrences: the spring floods, the river overflowing its banks, and the general apathy towards a Fourth of July celebration being the only constants in my ever-changing life.

For my parents, one positive event was that our old house finally received access to the waterline. The main supply pipes were laid during the fall, and they were connected to the house as soon as the weather allowed. Gas lines were the next utility to be installed, but there was no timeframe established. The taxes would increase to cover these services, but my father could afford the increase. In fact, he had finally accumulated enough money to purchase a larger house and lot on upper Center Street, right next to Hills' Tavern. The family moved into that house during the summer. This new house of theirs already had water and gas lines, so they wouldn't be missing out on these conveniences.

Father also purchased a house directly across the street from his, where Center Street and South Street converged. He offered to rent this second house to Sam and me. Aside from being physically closer to my family, this lot was further away from the hustle and bustle of Main Street. I convinced Sam it would be a good place to raise a family, so we took Father up on his offer and moved into our new house later that summer. Father charged us four dollars a month for rent. He easily could have gotten twice that amount but was helping our soon-to-be family get established. The rent was a little more than we were paying on Main Street, but we now had our very own home and lot.

In our new house, Sam was able to save some money after paying the rent and buying the necessities. We did as much as we could together that summer since we knew our life would change once the baby was born. In reality, my pregnancy had already affected our activities. I found that I was less comfortable sitting for long periods of time, particularly in the sun, at base ball games. And I didn't have the stamina to take long walks like we used to, especially up the Court Street or North Street hills.

On Thursday morning, November 11, I went into labor. I was excited, yet also afraid. Moreover, I was extremely uncomfortable. Sam had not yet left for work, so he rushed across the street to get my mother. She subsequently sent word for the doctor, and within minutes, both were by my bedside.

Labor was painful and lasted several hours, which seemed like several weeks to me. I was scared to death and just wanted the pain to end. I was aware that painkillers were commonly used during childbirth, but my physician was vehemently opposed to their use. Why couldn't my doctor be like Queen Victoria's, who provided her with chloroform as pain relief during labor and delivery? But eventually, the pain was over, and I was holding our baby boy in my arms. We had previously decided that if it was a boy, we'd name him Samuel Joseph. And so it was that little Samuel Joseph Carey entered this world on a crisp autumn morning, just two weeks before Thanksgiving.

We had a lot to be thankful for that year. The war was a distant memory, I was married to the man I loved, we had a new house, a new baby boy, and everyone was happy and healthy. Christmas took on a whole new perspective for me as well, and I took pleasure in my role as a mother and wife for the holiday. It was a joy to care for our own baby, and it kept me occupied throughout the winter. Almost before I realized, the snow was gone for good, the robins were busy hunting for worms in the yard, and the sight of flowers signaled the arrival of spring.

Monday, May 30 of 1870 was Decoration Day, and the village put on quite an elaborate tribute to honor the men who lost their lives during the Civil War. All the businesses were closed for the day, and most of the area farms had work suspended so that as many people as possible could participate. Hundreds came to pay tribute and take part in the ceremony and services.

Sam and I took young Sam in his buggy and walked halfway down Center Street to watch the procession make its way up to the cemetery at Temple Hill. There we joined my parents, Father having a rare day off, along with my younger brother and sisters. It was nice to have our combined families together for the occasion.

The parade began in the afternoon at the intersection of Main and Center Streets and was led by Fielder's Cornet Band. They not only provided a military cadence for the pageant but also quite an impressive appearance in their bright red coats and white pants. The band was followed by a group of surviving military officers and then a group of village officers in carriages. After that came a carriage full of flowers and wreaths to be laid at the cemetery, and a carriage of clergy and the speakers for the day, and about thirty-five veteran soldiers, marching in formation. They were followed by two very impressive fire companies and a group of young boys and girls from the Union School who each carried a small American flag.

As in the previous year's ceremonies, I mourned, in particular, the loss of my two friends Isaac Whitney and James Luce. This would be the fifth anniversary since James died, and Margaret McLeod, the young woman he was to marry upon his return, moved away over a year ago. I had not heard from her since but hoped she had been able to move on and start a new life.

After the ceremony at Temple Hill, the entire parade regrouped and continued on to the Catholic cemetery, paying equal tribute to the two soldier boys buried there. The procession then headed back to the Temple Hill Academy for a few more speeches. By this time, Sam and I had returned home with the baby. It had been a long and tiring day.

By early summer, it wasn't unusual to string together several days where the temperature never dipped below ninety until the sunset. I spent most of my time outside in the shade with little Sam, trying to stay cool.

On June 29, 1870, we were visited by Mr. Killip, who was taking the federal census. He was the music director and teacher for the village, but I also remembered him as a neighbor on North Street. That prompted my mind to drift back to the previous census of 1860, when I was an eight-year-old child sitting in a cherry tree in our backyard, watching the census taker walking door-to-door on North Street. My how things had changed in just ten years.

His visit was brief, and since Sam was at work, I answered all of his questions, which were simple and straightforward. Sam was listed as the head of the household and his occupation as "laborer." Since we didn't own the title to the house, but only rented it, there was no real estate value listed, and I estimated our personal property at about one hundred dollars. Our places of birth, as well as that of our parents, were recorded, and that completed all the information Mr. Killip had requested.

After he left, I thought about how impersonal all the questions had been. There was no real insight into us as human beings, no reflection of the joy or sadness, the trials and tribulations, or the daily struggles and happiness of our family of three. We were just names and numbers. The most significant question asked might have been "place of birth."

It was no secret that Irish immigrants in our valley were often treated as second-class citizens. Perhaps because the founders of our township were of British ancestry, we generally had a stigma associated with us that we weren't "upper-class" citizens. In fact, it was rare that one of our own even became "middle-class." My father worked very hard to overcome the perception that he was just another Irish misfit.

I often shared these feelings with our new next-door neighbors, John McCoy, and his wife, Elizabeth. Our approach to the prejudice was to do the best that we could do with the hope that our perceived character might be improved. The McCoys had also come from Ireland to escape the famine. They settled in Geneseo, as my parents had, and all five of their children were born here. Their girls, Bridget, Mary, Sarah, and Susan, were all under sixteen, and their son James was ten. I spent many days at Elizabeth's house with young Sam while our husbands were at work.

Further down the street lived a colored family: Benjamin James, his wife, Sarah, and their two sons, Augustus and Oscar. I suppose the Negroes in our village had even more right than the Irish to complain about how they were perceived, but Mr. and Mrs. James were very kindhearted and hardworking people. He was a stonemason, worked tirelessly, and they owned their own house. Their boys were very well-behaved, and four-year-old Oscar was just as cute as a button.

Across the street, and next door to Father's house, was Hills' Tavern. By the time we lived across the street, only three remaining daughters lived in the building. It would have been nice for them to have been able to maintain and operate the tavern themselves, but I was just as pleased that it was closed for business. The benefit for me was less traffic and the resultant dust, less noise from any rowdy patrons, and an increased sense of security from not having transients living across the street on a continual basis.

The heat we experienced in June carried over into July. Mr. Crawford began wetting down Main Street with his sprinkler to minimize the dust, but there was no comparable effort away from the business area. Any wagon or buggy that rumbled past our house kicked up a great cloud of dust that gradually settled over anything that was outside the house, including my laundry.

One Saturday in October, Sam had gone off to work with a crew that was painting a house on Main Street. I expected that he'd be home by sunset, but he wasn't. As the hours passed, my thoughts progressed from initial concern over his safety to rage over the likelihood that he was drinking in some saloon with his buddies. When he stumbled in the door close to midnight, not only was he still drunk, but his nose had been bloodied, and his clothes were covered in dust and mud, both front and back.

He and his pals had retired to Weller and McGuire's Saloon on Main Street after they finished painting for the day. They had been paid in cash for the day's effort and immediately decided to patronize the saloon to enjoy some cold beer, a cigar or two, and play a few games of billiards. As the evening progressed, a much larger crowd had gathered, not only inside the saloon but also outside on the street.

No one will probably ever know exactly what prompted it, but before long, a major fight broke out. The proprietors of the saloon managed to get most of the combatants outside, but the altercations in the street grew larger and more aggressive and soon involved dozens of men. Eventually, it was quieted down, and the crowds dispersed after the threat of spending the night in jail.

Needless to say, I was extremely upset with Sam, and I expressed my displeasure in a very loud voice. Loud enough to wake young Sam, and then he was crying as well. Ultimately, I got the baby settled down and back to sleep, but I was too furious to go to bed myself. I locked myself in the bedroom and told Sam he could sleep outside for all I cared. The next day, I refused to speak to him at all. I went to mass with the baby and my parents and returned to their house after the church service. We ate dinner with them as well and didn't return home until dark when it was time for little Sam to go to bed.

Sam did apologize to me for being inconsiderate, and he told me that he'd avoid getting into situations like that in the future. For the next several weeks, he was true to his word and returned home after work each and every day.

November 1, or All Saints' Day, fell on a Tuesday, and Sam took the day off from work and attended services at Saint Mary's with the baby and me. I knew he could change if he wanted to and be the man I originally fell in love with.

CHAPTER 13

Family Growing Pains

December of 1870 turned out to be a wonderful time for our family. I had saved enough money from my mending jobs to buy Sam a new pair of boots from Rose and Miller's store. They cost me almost four dollars, and I gave them to him as a Christmas gift. I had enough left over to buy little Sam some new clothes from Metcalf's store. He continued to be an absolute joy in my life. On Christmas morning, Sam stunned me with a large, beautifully wrapped gift. Just the sight of the paper wrapping and large red ribbon sent a feeling of warmth and appreciation throughout my body. With sheer abandonment, I tore open the package to find a new dress and a beautiful shawl, which he had bought at

Bishop's. He had kept it there until Christmas so that I'd be surprised. I was.

We celebrated a wonderful holiday that year, having a nice roast beef dinner with my parents. That was followed on December 28 by a gala festival put on by Saint Mary's Church at the concert hall. Sam spent the entire day with me; we had such a wonderful time that it appeared our future would be as bright as the new blanket of snow on the lawns throughout the village.

Young Sam was a healthy baby and kept me focused on being a good mother. The neighbor girls, Bridget and Mary McCoy, would occasionally watch him for me if I needed to run errands and didn't want to bring him out. It seemed there was no shortage of babysitters at my disposal. If it wasn't one of the McCoy girls, I also had my sisters Anna and Ellen, just across the street, whenever I needed them to help.

I looked forward to the springtime when it would be warm enough to spend more time outdoors. When May finally arrived, I attended the Decoration Day celebration as a proud mother. I stood with my father and younger sisters in the shade of a large tree overlooking the decorated veterans' graves as we listened to the orations and the band playing hymns. I was grateful for the shade because I had discovered I was pregnant again.

Both Sam and I were happy to be having another child. Sam was working for Misters French and Wilson as part of a crew repairing and painting homes and businesses in the village. Although the work was fairly routine, it wasn't guaranteed.

I had suggested to him numerous times that it might be better if he applied for a job at the American Croquet Company factory or the machine shop, as it might be more dependable. With a reliable income, we could better plan for our soon-to-be larger family. But he didn't want to be committed to a manufacturing job—he enjoyed the freedom of working with a crew outside. I then suggested that he might become a bricklayer. They earned about $3.50 a day. That was much more than he was making as a painter, and it would also allow him some freedom and outdoor work.

My suggestions fell on deaf ears. But as long as he kept working and spent his free time with little Sam and me, I didn't complain.

On Saturday, June 17, Sam didn't work and instead took me to a base ball game at the fairgrounds. Bridget McCoy watched little Sam while the two of us walked down to the field where I had first laid eyes on him. The game was a good one, the Hunkidory club from Geneseo beat the Lima club 34 to 27. The skies had threatened rain all afternoon, but it held off. That night, we received a soaking rain that continued all day Sunday. It had been extremely dry for weeks, and the rain was very welcome and a blessing for the crops.

There was quite a large celebration for the Fourth of July in Dansville that year. There were tub races in the canal, a greased pig, horse racing, and a base ball tournament with a silver ball to be awarded to the best club in the county. Although the Fourth was on a Tuesday, Sam had the day off and wanted to attend the festivities, especially the base ball matches. I did not feel like spending the day in Dansville with a young baby, so I reluctantly agreed to let him go without me. As expected, he didn't return home until well after dark and in a drunken state. He hadn't gotten in any fights at least, and he told me he had won all his "drinking money" on wagers at the Driving Park.

There had been a provision attached to the excise law that year, which allowed the wives of men who were addicted to drink the right to warn liquor dealers not to sell to their husbands. Those in violation could be fined as much as fifty dollars. Unfortunately, the fines would be collected by the towns instead of the poor wife, which would have been more just. Had that been the case, Sam would have been put on notice in all the towns of the county. However, I simply tolerated his favorite means of "relaxation."

In September, the men Sam was working for, French and Wilson, began work on some significant improvements to the courthouse and jail. Sam was on a crew responsible for painting the fence around the entire perimeter and actually seemed anxious to go to work each morning. Stable employment for him was important in keeping him out of trouble, and the secure income did much to ease my mind about how our welfare would be after the new baby was born.

As darkness began to fall on September 15, Michael O'Grady's young son began lighting the streetlamps along Main Street as he had been doing all summer. But he was startled when he approached Mrs.

Eli Bush's residence. As he began to light the lamppost, she threw open her front door, drew a revolver from her pocket, and fired two shots at him. The first shot missed him, but the second struck his leg below the knee. Bystanders immediately sent for Dr. Chase, who examined the boy and found the ball lodged in his leg bone. The constable was also called, and he arrested Mrs. Bush and took her off to jail. She claimed that she had warned the boy not to light the lamp in front of her house many times and was finally fed up. Apparently, she preferred the darkness, but she still had to answer for the assault. The boy recovered nicely, but I doubt he ever lit that one particular lamp again.

Two weeks later, Sam came home from work and told me that he was taking me to P.T. Barnum's show in Mount Morris the next day. The entire town was talking about this, and now I'd have the chance to see it in person. It was billed as P.T. Barnum's Great Traveling Museum and Menagerie. Initially, we had planned on taking the train to Mount Morris, but with me being seven months pregnant, he hired a buggy instead so we could be dropped off closer.

The extravaganza covered nearly three acres and was housed in three giant tents. The tickets cost fifty cents for adults, and since Sam didn't have to buy train tickets, he invited my sister Emma to join us. Since she was six, her entrance ticket was only twenty-five cents.

It was a thrill for her, and she also helped me with little Sam, although I really don't think he knew the difference between the animals in Barnum's show and the dairy cows in the field down the road from our house.

By the second week of October in 1871, we had learned of the devastating disaster that was being called the Great Chicago Fire. It had begun on October 8 and burned for two days before it was finally brought under control. By that time, three hundred people had died, most of the city had been destroyed, and more than one hundred thousand residents were left homeless.

Although Chicago was six hundred miles away, I felt as if they were neighbors and now in desperate need of help. That feeling was shared by many, and as a result, most of the citizens of Geneseo and all of the churches formed committees to gather supplies and send aid. Saint Mary's collected nonperishable food items, clothing, and tools, to be sent along with the other contributions. In all, several hundred dollars in cash, plus clothing, boots, shoes, bedding, and tools were promptly shipped off to Chicago.

Although the exact location of the fire's origin had been determined, the cause of the blaze remained a mystery. The fire started about 9 p.m. in a barn belonging to the O'Leary family. The most popular rumor maintained that Catherine O'Leary was milking her cow in the shed when it kicked over a lantern or oil lamp.

Another rumor suggested that Daniel "Peg-leg" Sullivan, the person who first reported the fire, had accidentally ignited some hay in the barn while trying to steal milk.

Either culprit seemed to be a perfect scapegoat since they were poor, Irish Catholic immigrants.[4]

---

[4] It wouldn't be until 1942, more than seventy years after the tragedy, that a man named Louis Cohn would confess to having accidentally started the fire during a craps game. He publicly stated that he had been gambling in the O'Learys' barn with some neighborhood boys. When Mrs. O'Leary came out to chase them away, he accidentally

The anti-Irish sentiment hurt just as much in a large midwest city like Chicago as it did in a small rural town like Geneseo. We felt the sting of resentment towards us and were reminded of it often. All we could do was be the best citizens we could be and live by our faith.

Just three weeks after the Great Chicago Fire, alarms went off, and flames lit our own night sky as fire-ravaged nearly an entire block.

At about half-past eleven on Friday, October 27, a fire destroyed portions of the Globe Hotel and several other houses, barns, and businesses. In total, six structures were completely destroyed. It was believed that the fire started in Luke Taylor's carriage barn, which was destroyed along with his icehouse and hogpen. Both of the town fire engines arrived promptly, but a brisk wind spread the fire rapidly. The firemen battled the blaze for over two hours before the many onlookers could breathe a

---

knocked over a lantern, which ignited some hay in the barn. This confession didn't surface, however, until after his death in 1942, when he also bequeathed a large sum of money to the Medill School of Journalism at Northwestern University.

sigh of relief and felt that it no longer posed a threat.

During the following days, it was estimated that the entire loss would be about $10,000, with Luke Taylor's loss alone accounting for about $2,000 of that total. It was subsequently revealed that a fellow by the name of James Scanlin had been arrested and charged with arson in the incident. Although it was nowhere near the scale of the Chicago Fire, and there was no loss of life, this incident seemed almost as tragic since it was deliberately set.

The day after the fire, we saw the first snowflakes of the season. At first, I thought it might be ash lingering after the fire. It was a cold and dreary time of the year. I believed it either rained or snowed every day for the next four weeks. But I was anxiously looking forward to giving birth to our second child.

I went into labor on the night of November 15. Sam ran across the street once again to summon my mother and father. The time dragged on without delivery. Ultimately, they sent for Dr. Chase, who arrived well after midnight.

As with my first, it was a long and painful delivery. I still did not have the benefit of painkillers, but it didn't bother me as much as it had during my first delivery. I knew that eventually, the pain would go away, and I wasn't as frightened as before. Fear of the unknown can be overwhelming, but this time I knew what to expect. By the following morning, we had our second baby boy, Michael.

I rested for the next two weeks, but I still hadn't regained my strength or stamina, by Thanksgiving Day. Mother was gracious enough to bring over some mutton chops and potatoes for Sam and me, which we enjoyed after the two little ones were fed and had fallen asleep.

Christmas was a very simple affair in our house. I hadn't felt like, nor had I the energy for, decorating the house, and we didn't have much money to buy gifts for each other, let alone other family members or the boys. I was regaining my strength and was able to attend the Christmas Mass at Saint Mary's, which was the first time I'd been out of the house since Michael was born. It was a beautiful service, and the church appeared splendid with the holiday decorations. I felt comfortably at home there, and it made me feel better about the lack of decorations at our house. I fell into a spiritual trance, gazing at all the candles providing such a soft, warm glow within the church. There seemed to be an aura enveloping everyone there. With the faint smell of incense still lingering in the air and the angelic sound of the choir surrounding me, I felt truly blessed.

By New Year's Day in 1872, I was considerably stronger–physically, emotionally, and spiritually. I looked upon the fresh beginning as a chance to turn the page on a new and more promising life. Sam and I had been blessed with two beautiful, healthy boys, and he assured me that he would work as hard as he could to provide for our family.

On the first day of March, Chester Dennis, a previous neighbor and friend, died from injuries he'd received a few weeks prior. Chester was a son of John Dennis, who was a very well-respected colored citizen of the village. Chester was the one who had gotten into a fight with my brother Michael on the train, coming home from Avon one night.

Chester was as well-respected as his father and worked at the Tremont Hotel. Several weeks earlier, he had been kicked in the head by a horse. Then a few days after that incident, he had fallen from the back of a wagon and again injured his head. Neither was severe enough to keep him from working. But on Leap-year day, he complained of fatigue and went home to rest. He went to bed and slept about twenty-four hours before peacefully passing away.

He was only twenty years old, and my entire family was saddened by the news of his passing. Sam did not share the same degree of grief since he still harbored some resentment from that fight years earlier.

On April 9, 1872, the Board of Health adopted new regulations that required each and every homeowner in the village to scatter quicklime or chloride of lime in and around every privy, drain, cesspool, or any place with standing water. It also had to be used in places where there were noxious, offensive, or unpleasant odors. Everyone had to remove from their cellars or homes any decaying vegetable matter. Owners of building lots were required to furnish suitable drains to carry away all such noxious substances. Anyone neglecting or refusing to comply with these regulations was subject to a fine of ten dollars for every neglect or refusal.

The long-overdue regulations were an attempt to halt the spread of disease, particularly spotted fever, which had recently been running rampant. I hoped it would work. Not wanting to risk a hefty fine, Sam made sure our house was in compliance within the week. I felt more at ease knowing that we were doing something to protect the health of our boys, as well as our own.

Spring turned into summer with little fanfare or celebration. On Saturday mornings, Sam would take young Sam down to the river to fish for bullheads. I worried about a three-year-old boy on the banks of the river, but Sam assured me that he was extremely careful, and our little boy seemed to enjoy it. Michael was still much too young to tag along, but it gave me time to be alone with just the baby.

Bullheads were abundant, and the river was much closer than traveling to Conesus Lake. The fish provided a free source of food and helped stretch Sam's limited income a little further.

The river had been a blessing to us in that regard.

Although there were no fireworks on the Fourth of July, there was instead a significant disturbance just over a week later. On the afternoon of the fifteenth, my brother Michael was involved in a fistfight at Parker's livery stable. He had taken the morning train from Rochester to Geneseo, and in hindsight, would have been much better off had he stayed in the city. As he was passing by the stable, he heard several derogatory remarks cast his way from the men inside.

Granted, there are a few Irishmen in the community who give the rest a bad name, but I feel it unjust to label them all as drunkards. My father was generally considered, I believe, an upstanding member of the community and tried to serve as a role model to the other Irishmen in the town.

Unfortunately, Michael, now twenty-five, had led a less than exemplary life. It's a fact that he was under the influence of some bad Cuylerville whiskey that afternoon, but when he heard something about a drunken "Mick" as he passed by the stable, he charged into the livery stable ready to thrash the culprit but instead was met by a barrage of flying fists himself.

We weren't sure how many men were involved in the attack, but he was beaten up pretty bad. No arrests were made, and the newspaper reported that no one knew the cause of his anger and that he was under the influence of benzine.

I really wished my brother, as well as my husband, would drink less and be a bit less likely to fly off the handle and into a fistfight. Instead, they just perpetuated the stereotypes.

Hopefully, my brother John, just fifteen and still impressionable, would be more like his father than his brother. I'd always felt closer to John than to Michael. Michael had not been a good influence on Sam either.

Sam continued to drink too much, but it hadn't affected his job. Although he was spending more and more time at Charley Weeks' saloon on Center Street, it was always after work or on his day off. Still, I'd have liked to see more of his earnings brought home to our household as opposed to the cash till at the saloon.

I was by no means part of the temperance movement, but I couldn't afford to let either the saloon prices or the

time away from my children rule my life,
and I wished Sam felt the same.

CHAPTER 14

Another Epidemic

Just before the first anniversary of Michael's birth, it began snowing. Although Christmas was more than a month away, I felt as if it had arrived early when some women from Saint Mary's Church visited our house one afternoon. They brought with them several items of winter clothing for the boys. It was a wonderful gesture and made me proud of the Catholic community I was a part of. They must have realized or were informed by my mother that money was a little tight in our household. With a toddler and a three-year-old, I felt blessed now that they'd have warm clothing throughout the season.

Early in December of '72, rumors began to circulate about the presence of smallpox in the area. By the fifteenth, it was confirmed that there were several cases in the village. Smallpox, also called varioloid, was an extremely contagious disease. There was no treatment, and almost a third of those infected would die.

The school was immediately closed due to the potential epidemic and would remain closed until after the holidays. By mid-month, there had been eleven cases reported to the Board of Health. Who knows how many unreported cases there were. And in whose house. Two people had already died from the disease.

The initial symptoms included a high fever, fatigue, and aches. But later, a rash would develop with flat, red sores. Those who survived the disease were left with severe scars for life, physically and emotionally.

It spared no ethnicity or class. Even the late President Lincoln had been affected by it. Apparently, he'd contracted it just before delivering his Gettysburg Address nine years ago. Although he completely recovered, his personal servant, William Johnson, was not so fortunate and died from it within two months.

A vaccine inoculation had been developed by Edward Jenner about eighty years ago, but its use was sporadic at best until an epidemic would break out, and people would die. By that time, the Board of Health would attempt to get as many people inoculated as possible. I understood that once a person was inoculated, they would have immunity for five to seven years.

Dr. Bissell firmly believed that smallpox could not only be prevented, but it could also be cured by vaccination. If every doctor were to vaccinate each case that came under his care at once, many lives would be saved, and they would possibly stamp out the epidemic in a few weeks. My desire had always been to have our whole family inoculated.

Without vaccination, the belief was that exposure to the disease could be minimized by wearing a small bag of camphor under the nose and placing a lump of asafetida in the mouth. Young Sam wore the camphor, but the later medication had such a terrible odor that he would not use it. I must admit, I didn't know if the disease itself could be as vile as the taste of this gum. There was no wonder why it was also called devil's dung and stinking gum. But until we all could be vaccinated, I kept a supply of these remedies on hand, just in case.

I did all that I could to keep my family healthy and prayed that we all would survive the epidemic. School reopened the first week of January after no new cases had been reported. By that time, the disease was confined to only a few houses and only one additional death.

As I turned twenty-one, I discovered I was pregnant once again. Sam continued to drink more than I preferred, but he worked hard and brought home most of his pay. I couldn't begrudge him spending a Friday or Saturday night with his friends at McLeod's Saloon. Maybe when our third child is born, he'd realize he should provide more for his family: more time and more money.

The cold days of winter gradually turned into sunny, flower-filled warmer days of spring. My pregnancy seemed to be much easier than the first two, and I was actually looking forward to having another child.

With the arrival of milder weather, Sam seemed more focused on being a good provider and had increased his work hours. In addition, he had been doing work directly for the village. In June, he installed two crosswalks on Main Street. One crosses Main at Center Street, and the other crosses Main opposite Shepard's shoe store. He used flagstones that were brought from Dansville, and these new walkways would be more durable, therefore cheaper in the long run than the old wooden planks. The village trustees were very pleased with the job he did and hopefully would employ him for more work in the future.

After several years without a formal celebration, the town had planned a large event for the Fourth of July this year. Unfortunately, it rained very hard on the night of the third, and the prospects looked dim as dawn broke on the Fourth. But by mid-morning, the sun came out bright and warm, and it turned into a beautiful summer day. Two fire companies and McArthur's Cornet Band came from Mount Morris and joined our own fire department, soldiers from the War of 1812, officers of the day, and various local speakers to form a fine procession. Speeches were held in the courthouse grove, and the shade was much appreciated as the day grew warmer and the speeches longer.

It was a nice day to be out and about, celebrate the holiday with friends, and feel thankful to be healthy while nearing the end of my pregnancy. The boys and I got a ride back home, which was much appreciated, where we had dinner and rested before the evening's fireworks display. By the time we returned to town, an immense crowd of people had assembled for the display, which turned out to be one of the finest in the county.

Within a month, our third child was born. The birth was very easy, labor was short, and we welcomed little Patrick Carey into the world. He was named after Sam's father. As before, my mother proved to be an immense help in caring for both me and the baby. Her support was much appreciated, and I felt somewhat guilty for the attention I received, knowing that she never benefitted from the same helpfulness following the delivery of each of her own children.

By the end of the following week, I was fully capable of taking care of myself and the baby, but it was comforting to know Mother was so close and willing to help. Little Sam was now four years old, and Michael was two, and both had become more independent, which was also a blessing. Everything was fine within our household and within the village. Well, except for the damn potato bugs.

There had been an infestation of potato bugs in the fields of the valley. They had become an insidious pest. Fowl won't eat them, and the application of strong lime will not destroy them. The most surefire method of eradication was picking them off by hand and killing them. This was hardly practical, however, for all the crops in the area.

I'm sure Father and all the other Irish immigrants who had left the homeland because of the famine were having dismal thoughts regarding the future of the potato crop in the Genesee Valley.

Fortunately, we had an abundance of other produce to live on and were not solely dependent on the potato for sustenance. But the stubbornness and dedication of the valley farmers led them to continue to search for methods to eradicate this new threat. One technique that had shown success was to sprinkle the affected plants with camphor water. This concoction was prepared by adding a quarter-pound of camphor to a hogshead of water and letting it sit overnight. When sprinkled on the affected plants, it would drive the bugs away, but it wouldn't kill them. Eventually, they'd make their way back to the host plant, especially after a few rainstorms.

What most farmers eventually turned to was the use of Paris green as a more permanent solution to the blight. Paris green was a highly toxic crystalline powder that got its name from its use for killing rats in Parisian sewers. It was being used more frequently in the U.S. as a very effective insecticide. It was generally mixed with ashes and lime and sifted onto the plants while moist with dew or rain. My concern was that because it was poisonous to humans as well, its use should be carefully monitored and controlled.

Personally, I'd rather have eliminated potatoes from our diet than run the risk of an inadvertent poisoning from these new insecticides. We were blessed in that we'd been spared any tragedies to our young family.

Our neighbors down the street were not so fortunate. Recently, Michael and Bridget O'Grady's youngest daughter, Maggie, who was only six, fell into the cistern in her house and nearly drowned. Their cistern was located under the kitchen floor, and apparently, the cover had been left off one morning. The large cistern was nearly full of water. Maggie cried out as she fell, and her mother rushed into the kitchen to see what was going on. Bridget screamed to her neighbors for help, who were just outside the open window. She then jumped in to save her child but hit her head on a beam, rendering herself unconscious as she fell into the cistern. Both would have drowned had it not been for the neighbors who arrived in time to rescue them. Fortunately, both mother and daughter survived the incident, but it could easily have had a more tragic outcome. Sadly, it seems a person could drown in their own house, far from any body of water.

The remainder of the fall season passed by very quickly. Taking care of three young boys and a husband who occasionally acted like an infant himself, was a full-time job. I found that I had no time to take in darning and mending jobs as I used to, and we were totally dependent on Sam's income to live on. But the time passed quickly, and before long, snow covered the ground, and Christmas was upon us. The boys and I attended mass on Christmas Eve, and Father O'Brien gave each of the children a special gift to take home. Sam had enough money to buy us a smoked ham, and our little family of five had a memorable holiday feast.

Sam continued to work directly for the village, and by the end of the year, rumors were circulating that the county would be signing contracts for improvements to the poorhouse. He felt confident that this new opportunity could provide a dependable income for at least the next year.

In February of 1874, at the Board of Supervisors' meeting, the committee representing the poorhouse and insane asylum convinced the board that the current facility was too small and overcrowded. At that time, there were fifty-eight people confined in very poor and crowded accommodations. The committee proposed enlarging the facility to accommodate at least thirty more patients. The proposal was approved, and a new addition to the present building, providing accommodations for seventy inmates plus a home for the superintendent, would begin later in the spring. In April, the sum of $10,000 was appropriated for the new construction. Sam shared the good news with me that he'd be fully employed and receiving a steady income to support our growing family.

The new buildings were completed within five months at a final cost of $11,450. A three-story brick addition was made just to the west of the original building. This new insane asylum was now considered one of the best county institutions in the state. Sam saved enough of his income that we felt confident we'd have enough to cover the rent and our living expenses for the remainder of the year. We'd even have enough to spend on leisure activities during the summer, provided Sam didn't gamble or drink it away.

CHAPTER 15

New Activity at Conesus Lake

In April of 1874, the possibility of running a regular stage line to Long Point during the summer was being discussed. Assuming the fare would be reasonable, I looked forward to seeing this idea come to fruition. It would provide those of us in the village easier access to Conesus Lake's cool waters during the warmest days of the year. I could envision Sam and me bringing the boys to Long Point for a pic nic and an afternoon of relaxation on a regular basis.

There was additional activity at the north end of the lake.

Beginning in May, a steamship was being built by Jerry Bolles of Livonia. The vessel, named *Jessie*, would be fifty feet long and sixteen feet across and would accommodate about one hundred passengers. He was hoping to have it completed and launched by June. To help offset the cost, he was selling two thousand tickets at fifty cents each, which would be good for a round trip on the steamer any time during the season. Although ticket sales were brisk, mechanical problems delayed the projected launch.

The actual inauguration was held on the first of July. People began gathering early in the morning at Mr. Bolles' establishment, the Lake View House. By noon, about three thousand people filled the grounds. About half-past three in the afternoon, *Jessie* was eased into Conesus Lake with much fanfare. With two brass bands playing, the festive atmosphere was not unlike a fair.

I was certain this would become a very profitable venture for Mr. Bolles. I had wanted to attend the event with the boys and be among the guests on the maiden voyage. Sam had given me enough money to cover the cost of the tickets and the stage ride to Lakeville. As the date grew nearer, though, I felt apprehensive. I had an inherent fear of water and just felt uneasy about being out in the middle of the lake with my children. My fears won out, and we stayed home and had a pic nic in the grove at Temple Hill instead.

My parents had spent five weeks crossing the North Atlantic Ocean to get here, yet I couldn't even cross Conesus Lake on a sunny summer afternoon.

Not much of interest transpired during the summer, and the boys kept me busy. Young Sam was old enough to help watch the younger ones, which allowed me the time to tend to the household chores. He was a tremendous help, actually, and I wished his father was a little more like him. I shouldn't complain too much, Sam had been working for the county steadily all summer and was bringing home most of his pay. However, I'd recently heard rumors that he had been playing poker with several of his fellow workhands and drinking companions. I worried that he'd lose money we needed to keep the house running and the boys fed. I confronted him about the rumors, and he confirmed them. I argued that I'd like to be able to do more as a family, but Sam contended that as it was his only means of relaxation, I shouldn't deprive him of that, and besides, he assured me with a smile, he usually ended up winning. I didn't want to start a huge argument with him and just dropped the issue, the argument, the lecture.

Some fellow from Massachusetts and Stephen Ayers, who was running for Congress, held a meeting on October 15, expounding the virtues of temperance and prohibition. A sizable portion of the local population was strongly in favor of outlawing all drinks. I had mixed emotions about the proposed legislation and could argue either side. The likelihood of people actually abstaining from alcohol as a result of this regulation was slim. It would only result in making it more difficult to obtain, and the quality of spirits would most certainly suffer.

On the other hand, I'd seen what liquor could do to a man and the people around him. It could destroy his ambition, his health, and his family life. And women were by no means immune from its effects either. As with all previous efforts, nothing substantial came from this latest temperance meeting, and life would continue as before.

Christmas was here before I realized it. Sam had been out of work since the completion of the new addition to the poorhouse. He had not made any money for over two months, and we had gone through most of his savings. Sam was not alone in his unemployment– lots of men were out of work, and even the smallest jobs were much sought after. To his credit, he did attempt to find work nearly every day. Having no income kept him from his poker games, but it also meant we'd have a rather simple Christmas holiday.

We attended the Christmas Mass on Friday night as a family, and the boys were able to get some small presents from the tree. Just being in church as a family on the holiest of holidays made me thankful for all I'd been blessed with.

The first three weeks of 1875 were so cold, most water pipes and cisterns froze, and water was difficult to obtain. A pipe burst at the Normal School and caused considerable damage before someone was able to shut it off. Obviously, the flooded areas quickly became frozen themselves and would have made fine skating rinks. But this forced the school to close until the situation was remedied. It remained cold right into February. On the morning of February 9, it was twelve degrees below zero, which was as cold as most folks could recall. One merchant, Mr. William Healy, had several thousand bushels of potatoes stored away and lost them all by freezing. With potatoes selling for just over a dollar per bushel, his loss was devastating. The only blessing was that the extreme cold weather might diminish next summer's crop of grasshoppers and potato bugs.

Dependably, the days grew longer and warmer, and before long, the school was closed again, but this time for the summer recess. Visions of ice-skating rinks within the building were a distant memory.

On the afternoon of June 5, 1875, we were visited by the census taker, Mr. Peter Miller, who was covering the 2nd District for the village. The boys were particularly rambunctious that day, and he could see I had my hands full with these three while I was trying to hang the laundry out to dry. He didn't seem to notice that I was four months pregnant, as well. He assured me he would only take a few minutes of my time and had only a few questions. He appraised our house at $800, and even though it was legally owned by my father, he listed Sam as the property's owner.

He asked our ages, place of birth, and Sam's occupation. I wish I could have told him something more substantial than "laborer," but basically, that was all Sam was. He worked for whoever would employ him, and wherever he could find employment.

I shouldn't have felt inadequate. Since early spring, Sam had been regularly employed again with a construction crew building new homes. There had been quite a boom in construction within the town, which was certainly a blessing for us.

Mr. Miller talked briefly with the boys, more as a friendly gesture than to gain information. I told him Sam was five, Michael was three, and that Patrick was two months shy of turning two years old. Sam and I were twenty-eight and twenty-three, respectively. He wished me well, complimented me on the children and condition of the house, and was on his way.

When the census results were published, I read that Geneseo had a population of 3,220 people in 1875, which was an increase of about two hundred from the previous census taken five years earlier.

A woman I had known briefly from church, Mary Britton, was found drowned in the river at the Four Mile Tavern on June 7. She had experienced domestic trouble and had recently been released from the insane asylum. She seemed like a pleasant woman, and I wondered what could have been the cause of her being admitted to the asylum. If she was indeed insane, why was she released, and what led to her death in the river? It was a sad situation and one that caused me to think about how her life could have been different. Perhaps I should have tried to be closer to her and offered more support and comfort, but I couldn't change things in the past.

Drowning still haunted me as a terrible way to die.

On Wednesday, July 28, Father took my sister Anna and me to Avon to watch our brother John play base ball. Mother watched the boys while Anna and I had a great day all by ourselves with Dad in Avon. It was a much-welcomed diversion from the daily routine of running a household and caring for children.

John was seventeen years old and played outfield for the Livingstons, a very successful team that traveled around the state. On this particular day, they played against the Brockports in Avon, and John was in centerfield. When he wasn't playing base ball, John was an apprentice blacksmith in the village. This occupation provided him with better than average arm strength, which enabled him to be a great outfielder and a powerful hitter. It was a beautiful sunny day, and I felt comfortable enough to stay for all nine innings. They beat the Brockports by a score of 18 to 0, making it a cheerful ride home.

That was the only game I attended all summer, but I was happy to have had the opportunity to see my brother play at such a high level and come away with a victory.

By September, my pregnancy was beginning to get the better of me. I tired easily and didn't feel well most of my waking hours. Fortunately, Mother was always close by and helped immensely with the boys. This pregnancy was, by far, the most exhausting of the four that I'd experienced. I thought I could handle it better, being a relatively healthy twenty-three-year-old woman, but it was wearing me down. As soon as Sam and the boys were fed in the evening, I'd retire to my own bed, knowing that I'd have another exhausting day ahead of me. Sam was very helpful with the boys at night and kept them occupied until their own bedtime. I told him how fortunate I was to have him around helping me. I think his sense of responsibility and my gratitude kept him home and sober more often.

On Friday morning, the 8th of October, I awoke to a layer of snow on the ground. It had snowed all night, and the wind was gusting enough to be forming significant drifts. Of all days, this was the morning I went into labor.

Once again, I was fortunate enough to begin labor before Sam had left for work. Having been through the procedure before, he hastily summoned my mother and Doctor Chase to assist me with the delivery. I was praying that things would go smoothly and, most importantly, quickly. And indeed, they did. By 10 a.m., I was holding a baby girl in my arms. After three boys, I finally had the daughter I'd longed for since I first became pregnant. We named her Nellie. The doctor assured us she was completely healthy and went on his way. Mother stayed with me for the remainder of the day so that Sam could go to work. The snow had completely melted by Sunday afternoon, and we had a very mild Indian summer for the balance of the month. The comfortable weather boosted my spirits considerably and allowed me to regain my strength, both physically and emotionally.

November turned unusually chilly, and by mid-month, it was bitter cold. On Thanksgiving Day, the temperature never rose above zero. We all bundled up, however, and attended the jubilee at Saint Mary's Church that morning. Even little Nellie, her first trip out of the house and only six weeks old. Father Donnelly led a beautiful service, and we all gave thanks for what we had. I had four healthy children, a home, and a husband who loved me and provided for our family. Sam had been working at the croquet factory since September and was bringing home a regular paycheck. We had a lot to be thankful for in 1875.

Feelings of happiness and gratitude were put to the test, however, by early December. It was announced that the American Croquet Company was going out of business and that all equipment and buildings would be sold at a public auction. This action was a result of the death of Samuel Finley, the major stockholder. Fortunately, Mr. Hudnut, the building owner, decided to purchase the machinery and declared he would continue the manufacturing operation sometime in the future. However, the facility would be closed at least for the remainder of the year.

Obviously, Sam would not be earning any money during this time, and since we were living paycheck to paycheck, it meant we would have another bleak Christmas.

December 24th began in a most disagreeable way. It rained hard in the morning, and by afternoon, a strong wind was blowing the continuing downpour in an almost horizontal direction. By early evening, the wind had calmed down, and the rain turned to light snow, which left the sidewalks terribly slippery. Mass began at 11 p.m., and we all attended–even Nellie. The walk down North Street would have been extremely hazardous for our family, and I was so appreciative that Father had hired a sleigh to transport us. Even breaking it down to two trips, with children on the laps of adults, the sleigh was packed as tight as a can of oysters for each journey.

It rained again on Christmas Day, but we only had to travel across the street to Mother's house for dinner. It was comforting to all be together in a warm house with a large, loving family. Besides my parents, the party included my brother John and sisters Anna and Emma, and Sam, myself, and our four little ones. Mother baked an enormous ham for the holiday feast, and with all the other side dishes, no one left the table hungry.

Although we were back in our own house on Christmas night, the festive atmosphere seemed to continue on through Friday, December 31. At the stroke of midnight by the town clock, every bell in the village began ringing in the New Year. Not just any New Year, but the centennial year of 1876. The pealing of the bells was the signal for the firing of cannon, which continued for an hour. Two bands paraded up and down Main Street before moving onto each of the side streets, calling out crowds of people. They even made it up Center Street to our house, where we briefly joined the crowds of revelers. Young Sam and Michael were very much enthused with the nighttime parade and party, but Patrick and little Nellie seemed frightened and wanted no part of it. Sam stayed out with the two older boys, and I retired to the house with the two young ones, but I knew it was hopeless to try to go back to sleep.

Although New Year's Eve seemed all too short and with so little sleep, New Year's Day was pure delight. It was a sunny day with a balmy breeze and a temperature that reached sixty-eight degrees. It was as mild as any day in May typically would be.

It seemed a perfect start to the centennial year.

We also learned that Mr. Hudnutt would begin manufacturing at the croquet factory again by the end of the month. It was rumored that all previous employees would be called back to work within the next few weeks. This was joyous news to us, and it appeared that Sam would once again be employed and receive a dependable income. It would have been far more enjoyable to learn that Sam was permanently employed somewhere and would receive an income that we could depend on so we would not have to go through these periods of poverty.

I had a more relaxed feeling of optimism by spring. Sam was working at the croquet factory and earning an income that seemed dependable. The children were healthy, well-fed, and clothed. The town was making plans for a gala celebration on the Fourth of July to celebrate the one-hundredth anniversary of our independence. Unfortunately, some sad news from the western part of the country cast a dark cloud over the anticipated celebration.

Newspaper accounts brought word from Montana Territory of the slaughter of most of the U.S. Army's 7th Cavalry Regiment at what they called the Battle of the Little Bighorn.

General George Custer and five of the 7th Cavalry's twelve companies were annihilated on June 25. Almost three hundred of his troops were killed by combined tribes of Lakota-Sioux and Cheyenne, estimated at a strength of over two thousand. It appeared the Great Sioux War would continue now with no end in sight. Loss of life during a war is always a tragedy, but due to the remote locations of these conflicts, as opposed to the Civil War, it seemed as if it was taking place in a foreign land and had little impact on our daily lives in Western New York. I didn't know anyone who was currently serving in the army, and hopefully, there would be no need to institute another draft.

The morning of July fourth was calm and beautiful. The celebrations had actually begun at midnight with the ringing of bells and firing of cannon. The cannon was set up at the south end of Main Street, but it sounded like it was in our backyard. It woke the children from a sound sleep, and Nellie was extremely frightened by the noises. The boys loved it.

The bright morning sky soon turned dark and threatening. As the parade groups were being assembled within the park, a violent rainstorm began that lasted for an hour. I told the children there wouldn't be a parade, and we planned on staying home for the day. But by eleven, the skies had cleared enough for the dampened participants to begin forming again. The gloominess did little to diminish spirits, and the parade continued as planned, down Main Street to the fairgrounds, where we met them. Once there, we joined the enthusiastic crowd to watch and cheer the sack races, potato races, wheelbarrow races, and other forms of lighthearted competition.

Sam entered the greased pig event and ended up the winner. He was so covered in mud that I would not have recognized him had I not known he was entered and won. The pig he caught was huge, and after being butchered, would provide my parents and us with a supply of ham, pork, and bacon that would easily last the rest of the summer.

The fireworks that evening lasted a full hour, and by the time they were done, our exhausted family had all we could do to make it back home and to bed. The moon was shining, the night air now still and silent as we each fell into a deep, sound sleep.

CHAPTER 16

My Own Failures

By the fall of '76, Sam had not only slipped back into his old habits but was getting worse. He frequently came home late from work, usually intoxicated, and had become much more argumentative. I couldn't plan a normal dinner and wouldn't make the children wait for him to show up. More often than not, the children and I would eat at our usual time, and Sam would eat whatever cold leftovers there were when he stumbled in. He was still working at the croquet factory, but he was drinking almost every day, stopping at either a tavern or someone's house on his way home. I must have been doing something wrong if he preferred this behavior over being with his wife and children.

He brought home most of his pay, so I was reluctant to make too big a fuss over it, but I never knew what type of mood he'd be in. I felt as if I was losing my husband and the father of my children. He was turning into a very undesirable mate. As fall turned to winter, he began disappearing for several hours on Saturdays when I knew the factory was closed. I learned from neighbors and some of his coworkers that he was playing poker with friends and future enemies at various locations throughout the village.

Initially, he boasted that he always came home a winner since it didn't impact the money we had available to run our household. But later on, there were more frequent occasions when he would lose his entire week's earnings in one afternoon, and there would be nothing left for rent, groceries, or basic household necessities. I was growing tired of making excuses to Father about why the rent would be late and if I could borrow some food for the kids. I believed both my parents knew what was going on and were just waiting for me to come to the same realization. Instead, I found myself drinking more than I ever had. Frustration and depression led me to consume whatever whiskey I could find from the horde of near-empty bottles Sam would hide around the house. But I always waited until the kids were fed and in bed before I started drinking.

I would drink until I fell asleep. It dulled my mind to the hardships I was already envisioning for our future and the choices I might be forced to make. I thought about ways to make money to support our family without relying on Father's generosity. There was very little mending or darning work available anymore. I even considered gathering fruit from the trees behind Father's house and selling a bushel or two to Birge's Grocery Store like I used to do as a child. But what was cute for an eight-year-old girl was pathetically sad for an adult woman. I still had too much pride to resort to such an endeavor, which I considered one step above begging.

The dark, sullen skies of winter reflected my mood throughout the season. It seemed as if my once happy life, family, and health were in a slow decline that couldn't be reversed or prevented, only numbed by whiskey.

Nellie's second Christmas was one of the saddest and loneliest days of the year. Our house showed very little sign that it was even a holiday. What few decorations we had in previous seasons were absent, along with the joy of celebration for one of the most significant holidays of the year. It bothered seven-year-old Sam the most. He showed an obvious sense of despair, and I felt helpless.

One day, I found him cutting a small piece of cardboard to fit inside his shoe because a hole had been worn in the sole. I had to turn my head quickly so that he wouldn't see the tears welling up in my eyes. Fortunately, the other children were still young enough to take it all in stride and seemed content with having a warm house and food to eat each day. Their older brother did a tremendous job of keeping their spirits up.

Sam seemed to spend more time drunk than sober and slept all day on the twenty-fifth, oblivious to our feelings. Although he was home, he was absent as a father and husband. The children and I spent most of the day across the street with Mother and Father and salvaged what we could of the holiday.

I felt myself becoming more depressed, and the long, dark, cold winter days seemed to linger on indefinitely.

Hopefully, with the spring approaching, fresh flowers and warm weather would help my mood improve.

At least I prayed to God that it would, for the sake of the children.

With the arrival of spring in '77, I promised myself I would devote more time to my children's welfare. I knew I could depend on my parents to help when needed, but I wanted to be a good mother to them on my own.

I had more or less given up the notion that I needed to be a good wife to Sam. He seemed indifferent to our needs as a family and sunk into a stupor of self-centeredness. When he was sober, he ignored us. When he was drunk, he became argumentative and belligerent. He had hit the kids and me more times than I wanted to admit. Lately, he was spending more and more time away from home, sometimes overnight. This didn't bother me as much as it should have, but I knew he was missing work.

I found out that he was spending considerable time in Avon, drinking and gambling. Some weeks he spent more time in Avon than he did in Geneseo. I don't think another woman was involved; he was too mean and drunk to have another woman attracted to him. My only concern was that he'd wind up dead somewhere. I assumed the nights he spent away from home were either in a cheap hotel room, some friend's house, or some farmer's barn on the way home to Geneseo.

Thursday, the tenth of May, was opening day for our village base ball team, and my mood had improved. My brother John was now a regular member of the Livingstons, playing right field for the team. Being an eighteen-year-old blacksmith, he had an arm that allowed him to throw a runner out at home plate from deep in the outfield, just as accurately as a pitcher could. On opening day, they played the Crickets of Binghamton at the fairgrounds. It was a warm, sunny day and I thought it would be beneficial for myself and the boys to spend the day watching their uncle John involved in a sport he loved and was so good at.

I took young Sam and Michael with me, while Patrick and Nellie stayed with Mother. Sam was almost eight, and Michael was six. The boys and I took a leisurely walk to the fairgrounds, and I could feel their excitement and anticipation build with every step. We arrived at the field just as the game was getting underway. The game was exciting and close. Fortunately, the Livingstons ended up victorious, beating the Crickets by a score of 10 to 8. John noticed us, and after the game, he brought us each a cold lemonade. Spending that beautiful afternoon with my oldest boys and their uncle John was as refreshing as that lemonade.

The children and I spent a calm and relaxing summer that year, just walking over to North Street and back through the grove at Temple Hill. I pushed Nellie in a buggy with occasional relief by young Sam when he felt I needed it. Michael and Patrick set the pace of our strolls. I knew it was good for the children but even better for me. But as summer turned to fall, the thought of spending the long, dark winter months alone again became oppressive to me.

CHAPTER 17

Hitting Rock Bottom

One late October morning in 1877, I awoke with a throbbing pain in my right jaw. It was almost unbearable, and the pain was relentless. It soon developed into a severe headache, which incapacitated me even further. It was a Thursday, but the boys were home from school, so I told young Sam to take his brothers and sister across the street to play with Emma. I told him I'd come to get them when I felt better.

I had to do something to dull the pain, so I filled a tumbler with whiskey, took a deep slug of it, and lay down on my bed, the remaining whiskey on the stand next to me. Gradually, the pain eased. I didn't know if the apparent toothache was subsiding, or if the whiskey was masking the pain, but I didn't really care as long as I felt better. I sipped at the remaining whiskey just to prevent a return of the excruciating pain I had endured earlier. Within a few hours, both the pain and the whiskey were gone.

Sam, who had gone off to work before my pain became unbearable, returned home to find me in a deep sleep. Looking at the empty whiskey bottle on the nightstand, he realized that I probably wouldn't be preparing dinner, so he fetched the kids from across the street and began fixing something for them and himself to eat. Sam mentioned nothing about the incident the next morning, which I thought was rather odd. I expected a fight that never materialized.

One week to the day after that episode, my toothache returned with a vengeance. I left young Sam in charge of his siblings and walked to Dr. Cole's dentist office, holding an apple-sized chunk of ice to my jaw.

He confirmed it was an abscessed tooth that needed extraction. He pulled the tooth and gave me a dose of laudanum to relieve the pain. I had never experienced such a mind-numbing sedative. My whole body felt limp, and my mind drifted away into the clouds, floating on a river of warm air.

Dr. Cole summoned a passerby to bring me back home in their carriage. The three-minute ride up Center Street seemed to take hours, and my mind was spinning. I did manage to make my way inside and into bed. The children were very sympathetic, and this time, young Sam took care of his brothers and sister and gathered some things for them to eat. His father did not come home that night.

The next morning, I awoke somewhat groggy but without pain. I prepared something for the boys to eat, and Nellie and I went back to bed. Before long, I realized the sun was high in the sky, and it was afternoon before I got out of bed.

The boys were playing outside, and Nellie was sitting quietly in the front room. Alone. She was hungry and needed to be changed.

As I was preparing something for us all to eat, I thought that I should probably purchase a small bottle of laudanum, just to have on hand if the pain in my jaw returned. I told the boys to watch their sister for an hour, and I walked down to Killip's Drug Store. He cautioned me as to how potent a medication it was, being a tincture of opium. He advised that an appropriate dose for me would be ten to fifteen drops of the liquid.

I brought the bottle home, placed it high on a cupboard shelf, and decided I wouldn't take any until the children were fed and put to bed for the night. Then, in my loneliness, I'd take a dose and drift off to sleep without worrying about what was happening to my life. It's hard to believe that only a few drops of that reddish-brown liquid could relieve so much pain and despair.

Sam didn't come home again that night, and after the kids were in bed, I measured fifteen drops of my medication onto a large spoon and swallowed it. It was extremely bitter, more so than I recalled with that first dose in the dentist's office. But before long, my arms and legs felt numb and limp, and I laid down and drifted off into oblivion. As I lay there, one of the last thoughts in my mind was that the next time I took it, I'd add it to some honey to make the taste more bearable.

When I awoke again, I realized that the sun was high in the sky, and the children had been up for hours. Initially, I panicked that they'd be late for school until I realized it was Saturday. We all could rest, and hopefully, their father would return home this weekend.

Sam did come home that Saturday, but he was in a horrible mood, and I could tell he was anxious to start a fight. I wouldn't let that happen and become the excuse he needed to disappear again, or worse, end up with bruises again. I also decided I'd hide my little bottle of laudanum. He didn't need another vice, although I'm sure his mood would be much improved on it, instead of the nasty belligerence of his whiskey-infused days and nights.

As it was, we successfully avoided each other for the entire weekend. I was amazed when he told me on Monday morning that he was going to work. Actually, I was surprised he even had a job. Apparently, he and a crew of fellow laborers were working in Avon, helping construct new houses.

I momentarily felt guilty about the way I had been treating him. He told me that it was easier to stay in the houses under construction than to travel back and forth between Geneseo and Avon all week. I agreed with him, and so it was that he was gone again for the entire week.

As Christmas rolled around at the end of '77, I felt myself sinking deeper and deeper into depression. Sam was gone more than he was home, money was extremely scarce, and I found myself sending the kids across the street to my parent's house more often than not. Fortunately, they were close, generous, and understanding. But Christmas would be a rather bleak holiday again this year.

I felt alone and sad continuously now, and the days were getting shorter, darker, and colder. Father made sure we had an adequate supply of coal and that our stove was working efficiently. Mother sent food home with the children when they visited. They wouldn't let anything happen to me or the children, but I knew they were disappointed in the direction my life was headed and the choice I'd made in marriage. There was an ever-increasing void in my life and in my mind. The easiest method for me to escape that harsh reality right now was to reach for that little bottle of temporary bliss.

I'd found it was much more palatable to ingest by dipping a large spoon in honey, making a small depression in it, and dispensing twenty or so drops of laudanum into the hollowed area.

I was aware that I was taking more than what was suggested, but I found that it worked faster and lasted longer at a higher dose. I'd find myself too often in a dream state, too lethargic to prepare meals, clean the house or our clothing, or care about what was happening around me or to my life. All I wanted to do was escape my poor existence.

My main concern became how I could get to Killip's every time the bitter liquid was getting near the bottom of the too-small bottle. My purchases were spaced far enough apart that I don't believe I raised any cause for alarm. Plus, each time I purchased a bottle, I'd tell them it was to manage my pain or as a cough suppressant for one of my children. That initial toothache was the only real need for it. Still, there followed so many more elaborate, imaginary ailments among the children and me that they could have filled a medical journal.

One of the nice things about laudanum was that it was cheaper than liquor. Being a medication, it wasn't taxed as an alcoholic beverage, even though it contained 48 percent alcohol, about the same as a bottle of whiskey.

January and February of '78 were clouded in a haze for me. Some days I was barely aware of who was even in my house. There'd be days when I knew Sam was around, days when I'd remember my parents being present, and, too often, days when I realized my children were all alone in the house with me. I wasn't fooling anyone anymore, and my parents were probably coming to the conclusion that I was as pathetic an individual as I claimed Sam had become.

I began to develop a haunted feeling that my kids would be taken away from me. The first step in that process, should it happen, would be to remove them to the county almshouse. Shortly thereafter, they'd be sent to Saint Mary's Orphan Asylum in Rochester. Many days I just cried when I looked at them and realized the world that Sam and I had created for them.

Fortunately, young Sam was responsible enough to care for his brothers and sister. My nine-year-old son had become a surrogate parent. But I also knew that my parents were guardian angels and had that innate sense to look in on us if they thought help was required. I no longer felt I was fooling either them or Sam with my use of the drug. I had finally admitted to myself that I was totally addicted to its influence, and I shared that realization with my parents. My mother tried to coax me into quitting and putting my life back in order.

My father tried to ruthlessly shame me into doing the same.

Neither approach was effective.

Eventually, my nightmare became a reality, and all four of my children were taken to Saint Mary's in Rochester to be cared for and were ultimately put up for adoption. I wanted to beg my parents to stop the process and take custody of the children, but I lacked the strength and the will to put up a convincing argument. I had sunk to the deepest level of depression I could imagine. That small medicine bottle contained a huge dose of apathy as well. My parents did not have the health or financial means to adopt four young children at this point in their lives and came to the sad realization that they'd probably be better off raised by more responsible parents in Rochester. Sadder yet was the fact that Sam, their father, did not seem to care what was happening and did not step in and take responsibility for his own flesh and blood. The only way I could cope with all of this was to take more laudanum. And I took it every day.

It wasn't until one early spring morning that I realized I needed to take drastic measures to quit. I knew it was spring because there were robins in the yard, I saw flowers blooming in the neighbor's yard, and there was a nice warm breeze wafting through the bedroom window. A window I didn't remember opening.

Although I could barely walk, I stumbled into the kitchen and reached for my little bottle. By this time, I had forgone the procedure of adding it to honey and dispensed my twenty drops, or was it thirty, directly into my mouth. I'd become accustomed to the bitter taste and knew it wouldn't last long anyway. Within a few minutes, my mind would become as empty and quiet as my house was.

As I became aware that the sun was setting, and I was conscious, I also felt the sensation that I couldn't breathe. I found myself forcing my body to breathe. It was no longer an involuntary function. What few breaths I was managing were very shallow, and I knew that it wasn't going to be sufficient to support life. I also thought that if I fell asleep, I'd forget to keep breathing and suffocate. I was alone in my house, and it would probably be days before anyone found my body.

So, I forced myself to breathe.

I came to the realization that I didn't want to die. Especially alone.

It would be easy to just stop the forced breathing and quietly and painlessly pass away. Yet, there was something that kept me breathing, and I made it through the night. In the morning, lying on my bed in a foggy haze, I swore to myself that I wanted to live, and the only way I could accomplish that was to never take laudanum again.

I began by tossing the near-empty bottle I had left in the rubbish. I began to cry as I staggered across the street to apologize to my parents for taking advantage of them. Too often, they had assumed the responsibility of caring for my children. Their willingness to help and their close proximity may have been the only reason my children were still alive.

I felt the cool spring rain on my face, blending with my tears. As I sat sobbing in their kitchen, I became aware of my dress and how bad it smelled. I was twenty-six, and I was humiliated by my appearance. I swore to them that I would change my life, even if it meant divorcing Sam. I couldn't blame him entirely for my wretched life, but he did little to help my situation.

My parents believed I could change my behavior this time. Perhaps they knew I had finally reached rock bottom. Within a few days, and with the help of some members from the church, they were able to get my children back from Saint Mary's. The children had only been there a week, but who knows what horror went through their young minds. Nellie was only three and probably didn't realize what was happening, but the boys surely were aware that they had been taken away from parents, grandparents, and the entire world they knew. I couldn't blame them for being so sad and upset. I was determined to show them the love that I'd been negligent in providing the past year. It was apparent that Sam no longer wanted the responsibility of being a father or a husband. But, with my new outlook on life, I really didn't care if he was present. I would try hard. And I knew I had the support of my loving and forgiving family, as well as Father Donnelly and members from the church.

I needed my life to return to normal, not only for me, but for my children's future. I gradually sensed that it could become a reality if I tried hard enough.

In May of 1878, my brother John got married. He married a girl named Mary Flannigan. Although she was of Irish descent, she had been born in Canada and moved to Geneseo eight or nine years ago. John was nineteen years old and working as a blacksmith. Mary was sixteen when they got married.

I was so thankful I had been able to abstain from the laudanum so I could join in their celebration and happiness. It was a glorious spring day, and I felt reborn. The nightmare of my addiction was almost completely blocked from memory. Sam was not around for the wedding, but the children and I accompanied my parents and younger sisters to church for the ceremony. It felt comforting to be part of such a devoted and caring family and confirmed I had made the right decision to fight through my addiction.

John and Mary made a beautiful couple. They purchased a house at 84 North Street, just up the street from where we all grew up so many years ago.

That summer, the children and I spent many afternoons at Mary's house, just to get away from our own home and provide a "destination" for us. Mary and I spent time preparing meals, watching the children play, and socializing with other women from the church. I felt proud that I was there, clearheaded, and acting like the responsible mother that I wished I had been the past year or two. I usually felt sad when it came time to leave. John and Mary had such a happy home, just like ours used to be before the children were born. There would be little food awaiting us back at home, not to mention a father or husband.

CHAPTER 18

Serious Trouble for Sam

Sam was spending almost all of his time away from home, in Avon presumably. He was probably gambling and drinking away any money he was earning. He provided nothing for the house, the children, or me. His world revolved around whiskey, the horse races, and the poker tables in Avon. He rarely appeared at our house, and when he did come home, he fought with me.

I had grown accustomed to him being gone and actually preferred his absence. I was once again taking in clothing that needed to be mended and was earning enough money to buy food for the family. Father was lenient with the rent payments, but I'd give what I could after I had purchased the bare necessities for our house. He accepted my rent, but very often, it came back to me in the form of coal, kerosene, or some other supply for our home.

It no longer bothered me what the neighbors thought about our situation, and my entire family realized I was better off without Sam around. Early in September, I heard a rumor that he had won big in a poker game and had the deed to a house in Avon signed over to him to cover the winnings. Further gossip confirmed the story, and I heard that the house was worth about $300.

On Saturday, September 28, 1878, Sam was back in Geneseo, drunk and belligerent, his typical behavior on the weekends. At about three in the afternoon, he entered Cullinan's grocery store on Main Street, where he encountered Michael Manlon, who was also drunk. Manlon was a mason by trade and someone who had lent Sam money in the past. He asked Sam when he would pay an old debt. This led to a heated argument, and when it escalated into pushing and shoving, they were asked to leave the store and take their dispute outside. They left the store and parted ways without further confrontation.

About an hour later, they were both back in front of Cullinan's store. Manlon asked him again when he would see his money. Sam flashed a wad of bills he had in his pocket, which were the proceeds from the Avon house that he had sold back to the owner just that morning. Sam shouted to Manlon, "You can see it, you son of a bitch, but you'll get it when I'm good and ready."

Manlon lunged at Sam and knocked him down in the street. Sam got up, drew a pistol he'd purchased just that morning, and fired a shot at Manlon's head. The shot just missed him, shattered the store window, and narrowly missed Mr. Cullinan, who was standing inside while watching the scuffle.

Manlon fell to the sidewalk in disbelief, and Sam, sobered by the incident, headed up Center Street for home.

Officer Rebban arrived at the scene shortly afterward, drawn by the commotion, and Mr. Cullinan told him what he'd witnessed. Rebban caught up with Sam just beyond Second Street. He immediately arrested him and took him off to jail. His hearing was scheduled for the following Monday.

After several delays, Sam ultimately didn't go to trial until the first week of December 1878. He was held in jail that entire time, which probably was the best place for him, sad to say. He wouldn't be getting drunk, wouldn't be gambling away any money he had left, and maybe could reflect upon how his life had spiraled out of control. He had sunk to a new low, and I couldn't even bring myself to visit him in jail.

I reflected on the situation myself, and couldn't believe what a monster he had become. My husband, and the father of my children, had become a worthless, drunken bum who had no regard for human life anymore. And yet, was I any better? It was not that long ago that I spent too many days in an opium-induced stupor with complete disregard for my children's welfare. Wasn't I just as worthless as he was?

I justified my behavior by telling myself that I was doing the best I could with such limited means. At least I knew I'd never resort to laudanum again.

At his trial, Sam was charged with assault and battery with a dangerous weapon, with intent to do bodily harm. Fortunately for him, the amount of whiskey he'd consumed had spoiled his aim enough that he wasn't charged with murder.

Sam pled guilty to the charges and was sentenced to six months in jail. Under an arrangement with Monroe County authorities, he was taken to the penitentiary in Rochester to serve his sentence. As he was being led away, Counsellor Abbott told Sam that he had been let off easy. He advised him to reform his ways and take care of his children, or he'd likely end up in the Auburn prison for two to three years.

I had mixed emotions about Sam being taken to the penitentiary. Although he hadn't been home much and was a mean drunk when he was home, he was still my husband and father to our children. I felt lonely for him being confined to a cell, but I also felt somewhat relieved that he was no longer a threat.

That winter, I found myself slipping into depression once more. I was drinking again, more than I should have been. I could sense that my parents were giving up hope on me yet again. I felt their shame, but my life had become so hopeless. The easiest way for me to cope with it came from a whiskey bottle. Resorting to the use of laudanum again was not even a consideration in my mind. Thankfully, that temptation didn't exist. I knew it would render me out of control once again, and I would probably die. My attitude was that the Irish needed only whiskey to fog their minds, not opium.

As 1879 began, I desperately wanted to change things in my life that led to such misery. My parents continued to help, but they could only provide basic needs. They made sure we had enough food to eat and enough coal to keep us from freezing during the long cold winter. The children and I wore our clothing until it was almost threadbare and often filthy. Our hygiene suffered as well. I no longer cared about my appearance, and with three boys under ten, cleanliness was not a major concern of theirs either. Nellie was just too young to know any different. I remembered the days of my own youth and Mother telling us children that although we may be poor, there was no excuse not to be clean. I just didn't seem to care anymore.

Even as I was living in what I considered dire circumstances, the county asylum had become overcrowded again, and work on an expansion began in May. With wagonloads of bricks passing our house daily, the dust fairly choked the kids and me. It was impossible to keep our house clean, let alone our clothing. At least that was the excuse I used for the neighbors. My parents knew better.

Sam was released from the penitentiary in June and came home to stay with us on a more permanent basis. He started working with his old boss and crew, doing odd jobs on new construction. Working on the asylum structures would have provided more secure employment, but once again, he insisted on the smaller jobs in the village. I think the ulterior motive was that he wouldn't be committed to a full-time, day-to-day routine, thereby allowing him to spend more time drinking and gambling with his cohorts.

He only came home to eat and sleep. By the beginning of October, I'd finally had enough of it and told him to pack what few possessions he had and leave the house for good. It took a lot of courage to confront him like this, but I had planned on giving him that ultimatum for weeks. With my courage bolstered by whiskey, I confronted him for what I hoped would be the last time.

He had been drinking quite a bit himself that day, and in hindsight, starting an altercation while both of us were intoxicated was a poor decision.

The verbal argument eventually escalated into a physical scuffle. He slapped me several times, and I threw punches back as best I could. This only infuriated him more, and he began swinging at me as if he were in a barroom brawl. I heard the boys screaming at him to stop, and my daughter was in tears. I can remember the fists flying at me relentlessly. I just wanted it to stop, and ultimately, it did.

I ran across the street to my parents, and Father went back over to gather the children. We left Sam alone in the house that night, and in the morning, reported him to Officer Rebban. After witnessing the evidence on my face and body, and with testimony from my father, he arrested Sam and took him immediately to the jail.

On Monday, the sixth of October in 1879, Sam was sent back to the penitentiary in Rochester to serve a sentence of ninety days for the abuse. He had only been out for four months but would now be serving another three months back behind bars.

CHAPTER 19

Sadness and Shame

On the evening of November 8, a Saturday, I had been drinking and fell asleep on the couch. The children were all still awake and had been reading to one another. Someone, and no one would admit to it, moved a candle too close to the window, and the curtain caught fire. They began screaming, which alerted not only myself, but also the neighbors, and an alarm went out to the fire department.

Quick thinking on young Sam's part kept the flames confined to only the window and surrounding wall. All the children began dousing the burning curtain with tumblers of water, and everything was completely extinguished by the time the fire crew arrived. We were fortunate that nothing was ruined aside from the curtain, the wallpaper, and my reputation.

The incident served as one more mark against me as a responsible parent.

The following week, with no money, food, or hope, it was determined that we all should be placed in the poorhouse and become wards of the county. The Friday that we were admitted, November 14, 1879, was one of the saddest days of my life. I was angry and ashamed, but I knew it was the proper thing to do. I felt degraded myself, and sad for the children who were innocent victims of a bad situation. I believed that if we could only stay a few weeks, with a warm place to sleep, food to eat, and a more stable environment, we would be home for Christmas and possibly start fresh for the New Year, even though we were adjacent to a lunatic asylum.

As we sat in the admissions office, my heart ached with guilt. They interviewed each of us for the admission forms, and I sadly offered the responses for the children's records since they were all ten years or less.

The last question on the form was, "What is the probable destiny of the person as respects recovery from the cause of dependence?" This line was completed by the admissions agent based on her observations during the interview. On young Sam's form, she wrote, "This boy is bright and with proper care might be made a respectable man." She obviously detected the untapped potential in his decade-old life.

On Patrick's form, she recorded, "This boy could, with proper care, become self-sufficient."

Sadly, and prophetically, the simple response recorded on my form, to the same question, was merely, "Bad."

We were given clean clothing, and the boys were taken away to the male side of the facility. Nellie and I were taken to a small room on the female side that would be our home for the next three weeks.

During that time, it was determined that Nellie, who was four, would be better off at the orphan asylum. The Catholics had three small orphanages in Rochester: Saint Joseph's, Saint Mary's Boys' Orphan Asylum, and Saint Patrick's Girls' Orphan Asylum. The authorities believed she'd have a brighter future by being placed in a new home rather than returned to a house lacking in food and bare necessities with two intemperate parents, one of whom was abusive and seldom home.

I had to sign forms to have her placed there, and since she was under twelve, they did not need her consent. The asylum would place out children as either an adopted child or as a servant. After a brief period of time, the asylum and the new parent(s), or master, would enter into an indenture contract concerning the child.

The indenture agreement stipulated that the child was expected to be honest, obedient, and behave. In return, the parent had to give the child room, board, and clothing. The child could expect an education, or training, if indentured as a servant. When the child came of age (eighteen for girls, twenty-one for boys), they received a Bible and sometimes a new set of clothing.

And so it was that my dear little Nellie was taken off to Rochester. I cried hysterically when I was informed of the plan. My anguish was diminished only after I accepted the fact that this was in her best interest. I begged my parents to take her in, but they refused to intervene this time. My older sisters each had their own lives, and it wouldn't be fair to ask one of them, or brother John, to adopt a four-year-old niece. I knew in my heart that I'd never see my darling little girl again. I prayed she would be adopted into a nice family and grow up in a more nurturing environment.

The boys and I were home by the beginning of December. I had a lot to make up for. I also recognized it would be nearly impossible to fill the void left by Nellie's absence. I worried that the boys resented me for allowing their little sister to be taken away. Patrick, who was only seven, took it the hardest. He cried many nights and missed her tremendously. My sense of guilt was at odds with my motherly instinct to comfort him. Meanwhile, young Sam was trying diligently to assume the role his father should have been providing. That was a lot to ask of a ten-year-old.

We were given financial assistance by the church and the county, but it was a meager subsidy. On Wednesday, the tenth of December, young Sam was caught stealing food from Pickard's store on Center Street. He had done this before, but this time he was caught, and the following day, he was committed to the Western House of Refuge by Justice Gearhart for petit larceny.

The Western House of Refuge, located in Rochester, was the facility where juvenile delinquents were sent. Now, both my husband and oldest son were confined behind bars in Monroe County. I sobbed uncontrollably as I watched young Sam being taken away. This time, his admission record, the second one filled out in a month, was completed by an official at the Western House of Refuge, not by me.

It listed his height at four feet, four inches, and his weight at sixty-six pounds, with gray eyes, brown hair, and a fair complexion. His clothing was recorded as "poor" and his occupation as "errand boy." There were no previous arrests or stays at a reform school or truant house recorded, but his brief stint at Saint Mary's Orphan Asylum was duly noted.

This reinforced my failure as a parent and deepened the abyss in my soul.

I'd lost two children in less than four weeks.

CHAPTER 20

Moving to Rochester

I began the year 1880 in a cold, joyless house with my two youngest boys. Nellie's life would now be different, and I continued to pray that it would be for the best. I began to think that possibly such a drastic move might improve my own wretched life.

Sam was due to be released from the penitentiary in mid-January. My plan was to move to Rochester myself, alone, and let him raise the boys in Geneseo. It was a difficult decision, but maybe it would improve the outlook for each of our futures. After all, I had already lost half of my children. Perhaps by raising the boys himself, Sam would be forced to regain the parental responsibility he had so easily abandoned years ago. I discussed the idea with my parents, and they reluctantly agreed it might be best for all involved.

I hoped to straighten out my own life, and with added responsibility, Sam could bring up the boys in a more stable environment. My father assured me he would keep watch on the boys and offer assistance if needed. I knew they wouldn't be completely neglected.

When Sam was released, I presented the idea to him, and surprisingly he agreed to it. He would raise the boys but didn't care if I was in his life or not. Apparently, the love we once shared had washed away like so much debris in the river, headed toward Rochester.

Before I left, I made sure Sam had a job and a place to stay. He found both within a week. He began working on the crew that was building the new addition to the concert hall on Main Street. This job should be secure and last him at least through the remainder of the year. He moved into a boarding house on Center Street with the two boys. Only then did I inform them of my plan. Father would rent our house out temporarily, with the intention of selling it within the year.

A few days later, I packed all the clothing I owned into a small case, Father took me down to the train station, and I left for Rochester. He was the only person I said good-bye to. It would have been too emotional to bid farewell to Mother and the boys, and I was afraid I would change my mind.

There was another federal census in 1880. I reflected back on how much had changed in the past ten years. My entire world seemed to have been turned upside down. Sam and the two youngest boys were now the only members of our family living in Geneseo. Nellie, young Sam, and I were now all residents of Rochester. I was in a room at a boarding house, Nellie was at the orphanage, and Sam at the Western House of Refuge.

At only ten years old, he may have been the most responsible member of the family, and ironically, he was the only one being held in custody.

On June 18, federal census taker Richard Riley documented for the government that Samuel Carey was living in a large boarding house on Center Street in Geneseo, along with his two sons, ages eight and six. In the same house were two other families, one black and one white, as well as two single boarders, again one black and one white.

A different census taker, Joseph White, was recording the families on upper Center Street. There he found my parents, along with my fifteen-year-old sister, Emma, still at home. Continuing over to North Street, Mr. White also documented my brother John at his house, along with his wife, Mary, and their new baby, Willie, who had been born in April. The Leonard households were stable and happy, and hopefully, the Careys in the boarding house would prove to be the same.

Young Sam, I'm sure, was not happy.

On June 15, 1880, he was recorded as a prisoner at the Western House of Refuge on Backus Street in Rochester for the federal census. His occupation was simply listed as "works in the chair shop."

At ten, he was incarcerated and making chairs because he stole food to feed his younger brothers.

The Western House of Refuge was a rather ominous-looking place, standing alone on forty-two acres. Like the almshouse in Geneseo, it was a cold, austere-looking brick building, but even larger and surrounded by a brick wall, giving it the look of a fortress. The main building, four stories high, was almost a full block long. The entire complex was surrounded by a wall approximately twenty-two feet high.

Also like the almshouse, there had been additions built over the years to accommodate growing populations. By the time young Sam arrived, he was among several hundred other boys incarcerated for all types of crimes.

I landed in Rochester in June 1880. I stepped off the train at the depot on Exchange Street with little more than what clothes I could fit into a small valise. I immediately felt lonely and vulnerable. In fact, this was the first time I had ever actually lived alone. I had gone from daughter to wife and mother in what seemed an all too rapid transition. Could I live all by myself and survive? I was slightly apprehensive but also anxious to find out. I knew I needed to face this challenge head-on and make the most of it.

Rochester was a dramatic change from my small hometown. It had a population of just under ninety thousand when I arrived and was much more diverse ethnically, socially, and spiritually. Yet, it had something in common with my little village that I could focus on when I felt homesick. The same river that skirted my birthplace, the Genesee, ran right through the center of the city. The same water that we used to fish in on tranquil summer days, now rushed under my feet beneath the bridges in the heart of downtown Rochester.

Still, I felt alone and out of place. It was as if an old tree branch that had fallen into the river along the banks in my home valley had now drifted aimlessly into an entirely new environment, amid all the other debris and detritus accumulated under the bridges of Rochester.

On a positive note, being in a more diverse metropolitan area, I no longer felt like a minority. Rochester had large concentrations of Germans, Italians, and Polish, along with us Irish. Hopefully, I wouldn't be looked down upon simply because I was Irish or Catholic. My social stature was more of a detriment. There was definitely a social class structure that was very apparent. But I knew where I stood, where I would probably remain, and decided to adapt to this new lifestyle as best I could.

My first impressions of the city formed during the last few miles of the journey as I stared out the train window at the unfamiliar gray streets and landscape. The terminus for the Genesee Valley Railroad was the depot on Exchange Street. As the train approached the city, I caught a glimpse of Mount Hope Cemetery off to the right. We then crossed the river and slowly crept by several coal yards and lumberyards. As the train began to slow even further, my anxiety began to rise. Did I make the right decision? Would I be able to live in this city alone? A sudden tremble of the railcar jolted me back to reality, and my thoughts returned to the cityscape that would be my new home.

Just past the Clarissa Street Bridge, the first of many bridges crossing the river in the downtown area, I noticed the Protestant Orphan Asylum out the left side window. My thoughts immediately turned to Nellie, and I said a little prayer that I hoped she would find a better life.

I thought about visiting the orphanage where she had been sent to and perhaps see if she could be released to me.

But I realized my life had not changed enough to justify another attempt at motherhood. Her future would probably be brighter without me in it. And I wasn't sure I could ever go through the heartache of losing her again.

The train came to a halt at the depot, which was adjacent to another lumberyard and the jail, situated on the west bank of the river. The boarding house that would become my new home was within walking distance of the depot, and since I didn't have much luggage, I decided to walk to my destination rather than hire one of the waiting carriages. It also gave me an opportunity to absorb the mood of my new surroundings at my own pace.

A block away from the depot, I crossed over to the east side of the river on Court Street Bridge. Two more bridges were visible to the north, one crossing at Main Street and another at Andrews Street further downriver. The Erie Canal crossed the river near where I was standing, by way of an aqueduct. I found it fascinating to see one channel of water overlap another via an elevated bridge. I recalled schooltime lessons on just how critical the Erie Canal had been to the development of our country. The canal was a vital link between

Albany and the Hudson River in the east and Buffalo and the Great Lakes in the west.

Also, in this immediate area, were several gristmills. They used the power of the river to turn gigantic millstones. These stones rendered the wheat that was grown in my fertile valley into flour, which was then shipped by barges on the canal to faraway places. This essential production provided Rochester its nickname: The Flour City. I impressed myself with all these facts that had never left my mind since my school days.

As I crossed Court Street Bridge, I came upon South Saint Paul Street, and one block further east was Stone Street, my new home. I took a room at a boarding house located at 72 Stone Street and registered under the name Kate Leonard. Sam and I were not divorced, but our separation and my attempt at a new life encouraged me to go back to using my maiden name.

My next challenge was to get a job. The obvious choice was to work right next door at the I.T. Davis & Company Laundry. I'd been washing clothes for free for years; I might as well get paid for it now. I should be able to make enough money to pay my room and board and have some leftover to save or spend on myself. If I found my earnings to be insufficient, I could make more at the Rochester Steam Laundry, just a few steps away on the same street. They did the bulk of the laundry for the New Osburn Hotel on South Saint Paul Street, but the working environment there was harsher and more demanding.

There was no shortage of dirty laundry in Rochester. The same amount of gossip and innuendo occurred in the city saloons as on the streets of Geneseo but on a proportionately larger scale. However, I'm not talking about that type of dirty laundry, I'm referring to the mounds of clothing brought into the commercial laundries every day. I used to think our family produced a large amount of laundry, but it paled in comparison to what I faced daily at the Davis Laundry.

The wealthy citizens of Rochester employed their own servants, which usually included washerwomen. But the majority of middle-class folks would utilize one of the many "send out" laundry services. Some used the simple "wet wash" arrangement where we washed the clothing, and they would dry and iron it. But most customers utilized the full service whereby their laundry would be returned to them in a "hand-finished" standard, which included ironing.

Being a new employee, I started out with the least desirable jobs. The ones that women with more seniority didn't want to contend with. My initial responsibility was at the bucking tub. This was a large vat filled with hot water and lye. It was used for laundry that was extra dirty or yellowed and dingy. Soaking in the lye did a good job of dissolving grease and loosening ground-in dirt, but it raised havoc with my skin and hair. I quickly found it best to pull my hair back at the sides and wear it in a tight knot in the back. Even with that precaution, I'd often find a considerable amount of my once beautiful auburn hair filling my hairbrush back in my room. Fortunately, within a month, I was transferred to work at the box mangle. This was a very large set of heated steel rollers used to press sheets, tablecloths, and larger items of clothing. It was hazardous work but much kinder to my skin and hair.

Working at the Davis Laundry gave me a newfound sense of freedom and self-confidence. I was earning my own living and not dependent on a drunken spouse. I missed my children, but I intended to straighten my life out, save a little money, and then move back to Geneseo before my boys became adults. My goal was to be back home within five years.

Things went well, and I adjusted to life in the city more naturally than I thought I would. Everything was close and convenient, with the exception of young Sam. When I moved to Rochester, I had every intention of visiting him on a routine basis. But the Western House of Refuge was on the west side of the river and several miles from my home. The Erie Canal, which ran just steps away from where I lived and worked, meandered its way westward and ultimately formed the back border of the property on which the institution sat. As I watched the canal boats headed west, I thought about them being within sight of young Sam within a few hours.

In the fall of 1880, I finally took a carriage to the facility to visit my son. Our time together was brief, but the visit did us both a world of good. I learned that he was scheduled to be released in March of the upcoming year, and we made plans to have him released to my father's custody.

On March 16, 1881, young Sam was freed and transported back to Geneseo.

A letter had been sent to Lewis B. Fulton, the superintendent of the Western House of Refuge, vouching for Father's character. It was signed by seven representatives from Geneseo, including members of the clergy, the police department, and the justice of the peace. It read:

> We, the undersigned citizens of Geneseo, County of Livingston and State of New York, certify that we are all well acquainted with John Leonard, a citizen of this place, a laborer by occupation, whose grandson Samuel Carey Jr. is an inmate of the Western House of Refuge. We know the said John Leonard to be a man of good moral character, of temperate and industrious habits, that he has a good house, and if his grandson Samuel Carey Jr. should be entrusted to his care by the managers of said house of refuge, we believe he would properly clothe, feed, educate, care for and discipline him and furnish him constant and suitable employment.

It gave me comfort knowing that young Sam would be provided for. My wish was that ultimately Father would do the same for Michael and Patrick. I knew it was a lot to ask of my parents who were in their sixties, but it was my foremost desire.

CHAPTER 21

Life in Rochester

Unlike Geneseo, where the river skirted the edge of the village down in a valley, in Rochester, it rushed right through the heart of the city. Not only was it the reason men first settled along its banks, but it also dictated much of the city's destiny. It brought trade, commerce, and manufacturing capabilities but often along with destruction and devastation. Particularly vulnerable were the two streets right along the river in the downtown area. Front Street ran along the west bank and the aptly named Water Street along the east side.

Front Street first developed as a marketing hub with butchers, grocers, tailors, and shoemakers. Water Street was home to more commercial venues such as gristmills, lumberyards, and coal yards. This was a logical orientation since the Erie Canal ran alongside the river on the eastside. Once it crossed the river via the aqueduct between Court and Main Streets, it headed west and out of the city.

Over time, the merchants' shops on Front Street were replaced by saloons and gambling halls. The vendors on the street gradually transitioned from butchers and grocers hawking their merchandise to prostitutes soliciting their own form of business.

In this central part of the city, Front Street on the west and Water Street on the eastside were soon known as Rochester's Bowery district. At one point, there were twenty-five saloons along Front Street, a mere four blocks long. These west side saloons catered more to the farmers who came into the city to sell their produce. The east side had its own share of saloons but at a more respectable spacing. There was actually less available real estate along this side of the river due to the number of mill races constructed there. A mill race was the man-made channel or sluice that transports water to or from a water wheel. Water was diverted from the river into that flume, and the current was swift and powerful.

Aside from my single visit with young Sam at the house of refuge, I never traveled more than four blocks and stayed exclusively on the east side of the river. My little part of the city had all I needed to survive. Saint Mary's Roman Catholic Church was within a couple of blocks of my home, and I attended it whenever I felt compelled to, although that became less and less frequent.

As I became more familiar with the establishments and people of the Fourth Ward, I was impressed by the number of people who shared my surname. Although none were related, there was no shortage of Leonards listed in the directory. They worked in a wide variety of occupations. There were tailors, coopers, clerks, shoemakers, tobacconists, plumbers, millers, grocers, blacksmiths, and hatters, all having the last name of Leonard. But it seemed the most common occupation among them was saloon keeper.

James owned one on Allen Street, John owned one on Front Street, Matt owned one along the towpath on the canal, and Peter owned one on Saint Paul Street. The first two were on the other side of the river, and I hardly ever ventured over there. There was something about crossing the river that gave me a queasy feeling in my gut as I watched and heard the rushing currents beneath the bridge. Matt Leonard's saloon was a place that served meals as well. I ate there often. But the place I frequented most regularly was Peter Leonard's.

I spent many evenings at his saloon on Saint Paul.

It was comfortable, safe, friendly, and within easy walking distance of my home. The occasional complimentary drinks for us regular customers made it even more attractive. I never felt uneasy walking home on Saint Paul or Stone Street at night. It was certainly safer for a single woman than walking at night on Front Street or Water Street. There were a number of regular customers at Leonard's saloon, and I had become acquainted with most of them.

For me, the saloon was a place to relax after a strenuous day at the laundry. It also served as a place to ease my feelings of loneliness and boredom. Many of the male patrons, on the other hand, had other things on their minds.

Whiskey was very effective at dissolving inhibitions. But the last thing I was looking for was a relationship. I didn't need another man in my life, and I didn't want to run the risk of pregnancy or disease with the likes of these characters. The regular male customers understood there was a hands-off policy when it came to me, however I couldn't help but feel a little flattered when a stranger showed interest.

It made me feel like a young, attractive woman again.

But as soon as their advances became too forward or aggressive, I let them know the situation. Despite the fact that it would have been easy money, I wasn't about to become known as one of the Water Street whores.

However, I did eventually garner a reputation as a woman who was not afraid to put up a fight when called for. I had been detained by the local constables on several occasions, primarily for having had too much to drink and not being able to make my way home. But there were a few instances when I'd actually gotten into a physical scuffle with a man who didn't understand the meaning of the word "no."

As a result, I also became familiar with the Blue Eagle jail, just across the river on Court Street. This workhouse was the repository of many of those who just needed a day or two to sober up or calm down. Those requiring a lengthier stay would usually be sent to the much larger workhouse on South Avenue.

CHAPTER 22

I Must Return Home

June 28, 1884, began like any other Saturday in my recent life. Since I didn't work on weekends, I slept later than I normally would. But the sun was already beating on the window shade, and I could feel the temperature rising within my tiny room. It was late morning, and I needed to get some fresh air. The air outside was already warm, and I decided to skip breakfast and have a light meal later in the day. I walked down the street to Washington Square Park, sat on a bench, and watched the city folk going about their midday business. Although it was shady, there wasn't much of a breeze, and it was beginning to get uncomfortable.

My thoughts drifted back to summer days spent in the village park in Geneseo. Even on the hottest days, there was always a comforting breeze wafting up from the valley. There were always shade trees to sit under or stroll beneath on every street in the village. There was always the sound of children playing and friendly townspeople nodding a greeting. There was family. There were neighbors to chat with. I couldn't find these same simple comforts in Rochester. I still felt like a stranger, and I realized I had not adapted to city life, and I probably never would. I missed my real home, and I needed to return to the valley before this city took more of a toll on me.

I wandered over to Matt Leonard's tavern on the canal to eat and plan my return to Geneseo. There was always a breeze adjacent to the rushing water of the river. It seemed cooler but not refreshing. The air had an industrial smell to it, not the fragrant valley aroma I grew up with. The sounds of the nearby gristmills were just as harsh on my senses. I longed for the sound of chirping birds in the backyard of my youth.

As I sat with my lunch as my only companion, I watched the canal barges headed west and thought about all I had left behind in Geneseo. I longed to hold my boys once again, despite the fact that young Sam was now fifteen years old. I had already accepted the cruel reality that Nellie would never be a part of my life moving forward. She was nine years old, and I dearly hoped she was in a safe, caring home full of love and with a future full of promise.

I missed my parents and wondered how their health was. I missed my brother and sisters. I had lost all contact with them after I moved to the city. I missed everything about my small hometown, except the gossip and disparaging looks.

I even missed Sam.

I had already given thought to moving back to Geneseo by the fall and not spending another winter in Rochester. As I sat there, feeling lonely and homesick, I vowed that I'd make the move within two weeks.

The heat, humidity, and the melancholy had given me a throbbing headache. I headed back to my room to take a nap in hopes I'd gain some relief. When I awoke, the sun was replaced by the glow of streetlights in the city street's twilight. The air, although still warm and sticky, was becoming bearable and almost inviting.

I felt the urge to spend the evening at Leonard's Saloon.

I was still feeling lonely, and the thoughts of my children and family had not left me. I needed to spend some time in the saloon to keep me from obsessing over the poor decisions I'd made.

As I casually walked down Saint Paul, headed for the saloon, my thoughts drifted back to young Maggie Leonard. What had become of the little girl who could spend all afternoon sitting in a cherry tree without a care in the world? Things were so different now. It felt like growing up had been a curse. But on this particular evening, I mostly wanted to escape my recent past and share my future plans with anyone who'd listen.

When I arrived at the tavern, I immediately headed to the bar and sat down on one of the stools near the end. There were a couple of regular customers, older men, who were sitting at the far end of the bar, but that was the extent of the clientele. I said hello to Peter, who was tending bar and ordered myself a cold beer. I commented on the minimal number of customers for a Saturday night. He replied, with an optimistic tone, that it was still early and business would pick up later.

After a few more minutes of small talk with Peter, and half a glass of beer, a young man entered the saloon and sat down at one of the small tables against the wall. I'd never seen the man before. Peter went over to take his order, and I heard him reply, "I'll have two cold beers and ask the young lady if she'd care to join me." Without thinking much of it, I walked over and sat next to him before Pete had even returned with the beers.

As the evening progressed, I learned that his name was George Lewis, he was a carpenter by trade, and he had lived in Rochester his entire life. He was single, had never married, and had no children.

I felt a strange attraction to this man and wondered who he really was and why we had been brought together that evening. Was this more than a chance encounter? I felt no romantic or sexual feelings toward him. On the contrary, there was an ominous feeling of danger in my gut, and I was cautious about what information I shared with him concerning my personal life. I began to regret accepting his initial request and asked myself if I should just get up and go back to the barstool. But I stayed and hesitantly answered his questions about my own life. I reluctantly revealed that I was separated from my husband and only temporarily living in Rochester. I told him I planned on returning to Geneseo in a few weeks, as if this were part of my escape plan. I mentioned nothing about my children.

After several hours, and as many beers, I learned that he was acquainted with my husband, Sam. He'd met Sam in Avon a year or so ago. He also told me that Sam owed him money and that meeting me felt like a good omen.

My suspicions had been confirmed, and my attitude toward him shifted to a more defensive posture. But the beers wouldn't let me walk away.

After rejecting several suggestions that he would be willing to forgive Sam's debt under certain conditions or there were ways I could pay the debt for him, I sensed that this encounter might just land me back at the Blue Eagle if I didn't leave soon.

Suddenly, I felt his hand on my thigh, and I realized I needed to get out of this situation immediately. I looked at the clock behind the bar and noticed it was just after midnight. Peter was preoccupied in conversation with a couple of men at the far end of the bar. I mustered enough strength and courage to tell Mr. Lewis I was going home...alone.

Peter didn't notice as I left the saloon. Outside, I headed down Saint Paul for home. Within seconds, I realized he was following me and calling out for me to stop and talk. I suddenly felt seriously threatened.

I saw the Young Men's Christian Association building at the corner on Court Street and considered trying to enter, hoping the door would be unlocked. Instead, I turned onto Court Street Bridge in hopes that he'd give up his pursuit.

He caught up to me on the bridge, grabbed my shoulders, and turned me around. He told me that I had misinterpreted his intentions and that I was drunk and in need of an escort home.

I pushed him away, and that's when his fists began to fly.

All I could see were fists coming at me in the yellow glow of the streetlight as I threw my arms up in self-defense. I felt the blows on my face and chest. I tried to fight back, but I was now up against the bridge's railing with my back to the river. Actually, we hadn't even reached the river, we were just past the canal underpass and over the race leading to the mills.

His fists continued to rain down on me, and I felt myself growing weak.

The next thing I felt was the helpless sensation of falling over backward.

The free fall seemed to last an eternity until I was abruptly jolted to a bone-shattering halt and felt my life rushing out of me in the swift cold water.

CHAPTER 23

Drowned in the Race

An article in *The Rochester Union Advertiser*, July 1, 1884, revealed my death:

DROWNED IN THE RACE

Discovery of the Body of Mrs. Samuel Carey, alias Kate Leonard.

While Frederick Wilson, an employee of the Ely Mills on South Water Street, was making some repairs to the machinery yesterday afternoon, he discovered the body of a dead woman floating in the race in front of the mills and under South Water Street. He notified the police, and Coroner Farley, who was in turn notified, had the remains removed to Milliman & Whitney's undertaking rooms on State Street, where it was identified as that of Mrs. Samuel Carey, or, as she was better known in this city, as Kate Leonard.

The right eye was badly bruised, and the mouth, nose, and ears were stained with blood, and one lip was frightfully swollen, and the appearance of the body was as if it had not been many hours in the water. The most rational supposition as to the cause of death is that she either fell into the feeder when intoxicated or jumped in with a desire to commit suicide.

About 10 years ago, she married a carpenter named Samuel Carey in Geneseo, with whom it is stated she quarreled and was beaten by him until she resolved to run away. When she came to Rochester last March, she is said to have deserted her husband and 2 children and to have pursued the paths of vice ever since, her favorite resorts being the St. Paul Street saloons. She was seen last Saturday night about 11:00 on St.

Paul Street with a young man, and both were intoxicated. The inquest was commenced at 2:00 this afternoon.

And two days later, after word had reached Geneseo, the local newspaper, the *Livingston Republican*, July 3, 1884, published this article:

Kate Carey Drowned

The Rochester papers of Tuesday gave an account of the finding of the body of a woman in the race of South Water Street near the Ely Mills. The water had been drawn off for the purpose of making repairs and Frederick Wilson, one of the owners of the mill, looking underneath for obstructions to the water, discovered the body. When discovered, the arms were twined around a post as if clinging to it.

The coroner was notified, and the body was taken to an undertaker's room where an inquest was held Tuesday. The remains were identified as those of Kate Carey, a daughter of John Leonard of this village, [sic who was born before he emigrated] but lived here nearly all of her life.

Twelve or fifteen years ago, when she was quite young, she married Sam Carey and was the mother of several children. Their married life was not happy, both being of intemperate habits, and the husband going one way and the wife another, the children meanwhile staying with Mrs. Carey's father and mother, where they are at present.

Mrs. Carey went to Rochester about 4 years ago and has been in bad company since. She was last seen alive Saturday evening at a saloon on South St. Paul Street in company with a young man whose name was not learned. The couple left the saloon together, both partially intoxicated, and had been quarrelsome during the evening.

In her younger days, Mrs. Carey was a fine and good-looking woman, and no doubt suffered a great deal of abuse, which probably was largely the cause of her reckless conduct. Her habits for the last few years naturally led her to an unhappy death. The verdict of the jury at the inquest was that she came to her death by some unknown means, and that she was last seen in the company of an unknown man on Saturday night last. It was learned after the inquest, that a man was seen about 12 o'clock Saturday night standing on Court Street Bridge with a woman answering Mrs. Carey's description. Probably it was the same man seen with her in Leonard's Saloon. The case should be further investigated.

Within a matter of hours, my name had been forgotten, or at least misspelled, and the facts became obscured. It was apparent that justice would not be forthcoming, as this was the last mention of my life in Rochester.

There was one follow-up article in *The Rochester Union Advertiser*, July 2, 1884:

<u>CORONER'S JURY VERDICT</u>

In The Case of Kate Cory, Whose Body Was Found in the Race.

This afternoon at the undertaking rooms of Williamson & Whitney, Coroner Farley held an inquest in the case of Kate Leonard, alias Cory. Mrs. Mary Ann Bristol, of Geneseo, testified that she had been in the city during the past week and recognized the body as that of Mrs. Kate Cory; did not know where her husband is now; saw Mrs. Cory at Leonard's on South St. Paul Street, where she showed signs of having drank some.

Deceased had been a reckless woman and was in the workhouse up to last Thursday. Peter J. Leonard, who keeps the saloon, testified that deceased was in his place, at 155 South St. Paul Street, last Saturday night, where she drank some ale and porter and left with a young man whose first name was George at 12 o'clock.

Coroner Farley stated that he had examined the body and found no marks of violence.

The verdict of the jury was that she came to her death by some unknown means, her body having been found June 30th, 1884, in the mill race at Ely's Mill, Rochester, N.Y., that she was last seen alive in company with an unknown man Saturday night last at about 12 o'clock.

Coroner Farley stated that he should see that the case be investigated by detectives.

CHAPTER 24

Taken by the River

And so it was that after thirty-two years of life, my soul had been taken by the river. That same lazy river that meandered through my birthplace and, just like me, ended up in Rochester, had drained the life from me.

My body was hastily buried on July 2, 1884, in the public grounds of Mount Hope Cemetery in Rochester, New York. This cemetery lies on the eastern bank of the Genesee River, just a mile and a half upriver from where I died. With no one willing to claim my body, or transport it back to Geneseo, I was buried in an unmarked grave among Rochester's other paupers and castaways.

CHAPTER 25

Aftermath

My husband's behavior and lifestyle had deteriorated to such an extent that he was admitted to the Livingston County Poorhouse on October 8, 1886, at the age of forty-eight, two years after my death.

My parents had taken custody of our sons long before this point.

The final remark on Sam's admittance form read: "This man is very intemperate, spends all his earnings for liquor, his health is entirely broken down by the use of liquor."

His health continued to fail, and on December 7, 1886, he was discharged from the Livingston County Poorhouse and sent to the Monroe County Almshouse in Rochester. There he was diagnosed with tuberculosis and transferred to the Monroe County Hospital, where he died at 8 p.m. on January 8, 1887. Two days later, his body was buried in the public section of Holy Sepulchre Cemetery in Rochester.

As with me, no one claimed his body, and he was also laid to rest in an unmarked grave.

Ironically, his body was interred less than six miles away from mine, both in unmarked graves in Rochester, far away from our hometown and happy life together.

We were closer in death than we had been during the last several years of our marriage.

My parents lived fourteen years after my death. My mother's vision had gradually deteriorated, and she ultimately became blind. On January 26, 1898, she passed away in her home in Geneseo at the age of seventy-five. Within three months, my father was also dead at seventy-seven. My son Patrick had been staying with him at his house since Father had been suffering from heart disease. In the early morning hours of April 20, he died peacefully in his bed from pneumonia, with Patrick by his side.

Patrick was married at this time and had a young son, George. Patrick had married a woman from Leicester named Della Mae Luce. They would go on to have three more children—Nellie, John, and Mary—after my father passed. Patrick worked for the Sterling Salt Company, at the mine in Cuylerville. On the afternoon of August 28, 1907, he collapsed on the street from heart failure at the age of thirty-four. He was buried in Leicester, New York.

My son Michael had not fared as well as his brother. He never married or had children. By age twenty-four, he had become so ill with tuberculosis, he could no longer work and was admitted to the Livingston County Poorhouse on September 30, 1895. He was deemed incurable, and on December 23, he succumbed to the disease. He had purchased a plot at Saint Mary's Cemetery in Geneseo and was laid to rest there, but there was no money for a monument. One more family member buried in an unmarked grave. But at least he is resting in Geneseo and had his brothers at his funeral.

My eldest son, Samuel, fared the best of the family, as I would have predicted. At twenty-seven, he married Della Mae Luce's older sister Mary Elizabeth Luce. They had four children, two boys and two girls. Leo, George, Catherine, and Elizabeth Carey were all born in Geneseo and had long, productive lives.

Della Mae and Mary Elizabeth Luce were the nieces of James Luce, who died in 1865 in the Confederate prison camp.

Samuel, the boy who had been sent to the Western House of Refuge for stealing, went on to become the deputy sheriff of Livingston County.

He died July 27, 1927, at his home on North Street in Geneseo, right next door to the house I grew up in.

So many things in this world have a tendency to come full circle. Like the clouds that form from evaporated water over a lake, later falling as raindrops on the brooks and streams that lead into rivers and back into that same lake. Likewise, our souls return to impart thoughts and emotions into others who come long after we have departed this earth.

"All the rivers run into the sea; yet the sea is not full; unto the place from whence the rivers come, thither they return again."
Ecclesiastes 1:7

Epilogue

According to Greek mythology, there were five great rivers that formed the boundary between earth and the underworld. The rivers Styx, Lethe, Acheron, Phlegethon, and Cocytus all converge at the center of the underworld, forming an infinite marsh.

It was believed the river Lethe, also known as the river of unmindfulness, cast forgetfulness on anyone drinking from it. The dead were required to drink the waters of the Lethe to forget their earthly life. Souls were made to drink from this river before being reincarnated, so they would not remember their past lives.

The river Acheron was known as the river of woe. Charon, the ferryman of Hades, would ferry the newly dead across this river to enter the underworld. Those souls who could not pay Charon's fee, or those whose bodies were left unburied, were forced to wander the banks of the river for one hundred years.

The river Styx, which Dante refers to as the fifth circle of hell, had even grimmer repercussions. Those souls unable to pay Charon's toll were punished by being drowned in the muddy waters for eternity.

Although Kate was Irish, not Greek, most cultures believe there is a mythical connection between the earth and the "otherworld" by means of various waterways. It's plausible since still water is a reflection of the world around us. The surface of a lake mirrors the sky, the mountains, the trees and everything else surrounding it. Yet, if a person slipped beneath its surface for very long, all that could be retrieved would be the vacant shell of a body. Its spirit or soul would have vanished somewhere into the liquid, perhaps to become a part of it. In the Celtic world, treasures were often thrown into hallowed lakes and rivers as offerings to the gods that dwelt within.

The longest river in Ireland is the Shannon (Irish: Abha na Sionainne). It cuts across the verdant landscape for about 224 miles before emptying into the Atlantic Ocean. This river, like many others in

Ireland, is associated with, and named after, a goddess. According to legend, the River Shannon is one of Ireland's "rivers of knowledge" and is said to originate at Connla's Well. The goddess Sionann went to this well to find wisdom, despite being warned not to approach it. As she drank from it, the waters of the well rose up, burst into a torrent, and carried her out to sea, drowning her there. Thus, the River Shannon was formed. The goddess Sionann merged into the river and became its very essence.

Kate was no goddess, but she deserved a fate better than what befell her. Who knows how her life may have differed had she not fallen in love with Sam Carey. She may have remained in Geneseo and become a productive and respected member of the community, such as her son Sam did. Instead, she was beaten by a drunken stranger and swallowed up by rushing waters on a lonely summer night. And being destitute, without the funds to pay the ferryman Charon, who knows how long her soul lingered on the banks of the Genesee River or the knolls of Mount Hope Cemetery. It's a shame that her body couldn't have been returned to the fertile

Genesee Valley in which she was born, but her parents had done all they could for her.

In July 2008, I placed a small headstone on her grave, 124 years after her death. This documentary and that marker hopefully provide some closure for her soul.

Rest in peace, Kate.

"The river flows, It flows to the sea, Wherever that river goes, That's where I want to be.

Flow river flow, Let your waters wash down, Take me from this road, To some other town.

All [she] wanted, Was to be free, And that's the way, It turned out to be.

Flow river flow, Let your waters wash down, Take me from this road, To some other town."

"Ballad of Easy Rider," written by Roger McGuinn (with a little help from Bob Dylan)

Postscript

The photo on the front cover is of the Genesee River between Geneseo and Avon, headed north.

The photo on the back cover is of the Genesee River as it flows under Court Street Bridge in Rochester, New York, approximately where Kate had fallen in. The bridge is much the same as it would have been in 1884, and remnants of the mill race can be seen to the left of the river.

Acknowledgements

First, I'd like to acknowledge both my mother, Betty Smith, and my grandfather, Leo Carey, for instilling in me the creative inspiration to even attempt this adventure.

I'd also like to acknowledge Frank Gillespie of The Friends of Mount Hope Cemetery for helping me locate Kate's grave.

In addition, I'd like to thank Michelle Saint-Germain and Jen Alcyone for generously offering their time and suggestions in getting this project to a point where it could be published.

I also want to recognize Ashley Martin of Twin Tweaks Editing for her helpful suggestions and editing expertise, as well as Madison Lux for her graphic design talent, incorporating my photographs onto the covers of the book.

Bibliography

Newspapers

Livingston Republican: 1860 to 1907

The Rochester Union Advertiser: July, 1884

Internet

Geneseoapog.org

NYShistoricnewspapers.org

Wikipedia.com

Ancestory.com

Historicmapworks.com

Rochester.lib.ny.us

Geneseony.com

Decodedpast.com

Transceltic.com

Aliisaacstoryteller.com

About the Author

Thom Smith, the great-grandson of Sam Carey Jr. was born and raised in Geneseo, New York. After graduating from high school there, he attended both Alfred State College and Rochester Institute of Technology, receiving a Bachelor of Science degree in organic chemistry. He worked as a research chemist for the Eastman Kodak Company in Rochester, New York, for thirty-seven years and obtained over twenty-five patents. His interests include travel, genealogy, photography, painting, woodworking, golf and curling. He currently lives in Spencerport, New York, with his wife, Patty.

CPSIA information can be obtained
at www.ICGtesting.com
Printed in the USA
FSHW010405130920
73330FS